Mastering Masters Swimming

by
George Bole

Published by
Swimming Support Syndicate
1739 East Carson Street
Suite 1650
Pittsburgh, PA 15203

toll free: 800-869-0758
office: 412-481-2497
fax: 412-481-2540

ISBN: 1-878602-37-3
Retail price: $14.95 USA
£10.50 UK

Cover photo shows Jayne Lambke

George's student goes for Gold!

Cover photo is of a Jayne Lambke, 51, who holds the Masters World Records in the 50 meter and 100 meter short course fly events. Jayne is coached by George Bole, and she holds many other short and long course Masters titles. When she set the World Record for 10K Swim, she broke the previous record by 2 hours and 49 minutes.

Parts of this book were reprinted from another book previously written by George Bole in 1984 with the cooperation of Arena in the U.K. That book is out of print, and it was called, *Drill for Skill in Swimming*.

The quotes and motivational messages found in the book were obtained from the book, *Putting Words In Your Mouth*, edited by Skip Bird and published by the Sports Support Syndicate. Skip Bird is a swimming coach and high school English teacher in Indiana.

 The author, Coach George Bole, has many friends and followers around the world. This book is easily exported from the USA. We encourage swimmers and coaches of other countries, and perhaps of other languages, to examine, discuss and utilize the following plans. The workouts are easily understood by those who are not proficient in the English language.

TABLE OF CONTENTS

About the Author

George Bole - Swim Coach
A.S.C.A. Advanced Masters Qualified Coach

Age: 74

Education & Certification:
1959-1963: Studied teaching and advanced teaching under Max Madders at England University-Birmingham; past director of swimming for the Amateur Swimming Association (ASA) in England. Gained the ASA Teacher's Certificate in 1958. Gained the ASA Advanced Teacher's Certificate in 1959.

1964: Loughborough College of Physical Education. Studied coaching under A.D. Kinnear, senior national technical officer of ASA. Gained ASA National Coach's Certificate.

Selected Experience:
1965: Founded the British Swim Coaches Association (BSCA).

1965-1972: Acted as secretary of the BSCA and was editor of the quarterly *Swimming Coach*, technical journal of the BSCA.

1965-1968: Assistant Coach for Top Elite -- the 15 top British swimmers (special training camps, Crystal Palace, London).
Assistant coach for Elite 30 -- the best junior swimmers in Great Britain at Loughborough College. Wrote a regular column, "The Coach's Corner," for *The Swimming Times*, a magazine published in England.

1965-1970: Wrote articles for *Swimming World* and *Swimming Technique* -- magazines published in the United States. Writer for *Krol* -- a magazine published in Spain.

1970: Convened inaugural meeting of the Federation of the European

Coaching Association at Barcelona, Spain. Elected vice president of the European Coaches Federation.

1972: Coached Olympic team at Gormanstown (Dublin, Ireland).

1984: Assisted with the British Olympic squad in La Jolla, California. Worked as a coach for Don Gambril, USA Olympic Swim Coach (1984), at the swim camps at the University of Alabama. Directed Gambril's First Masters' Swim Camp.

1984 to present: Coach for the St. Petersburg, Florida Masters Swim Team. Head coach in 1988 for Holmes Lumber Jax select team from Florida that includes several 1984 Olympic champions. The team competed at the World Masters Swimming Championships, Brisbane, Australia.

Honors:
1968: Elected as First Fellow of BSCA for special services in aid of International and British coaching.
1987: Granted the first life membership of the BSCA.

Publication:
Bole, G. (1984). *Drill for Skill in Swimming*. Cleveland, UK: Arena.

Produced:
Olympic Swimmer, 1972
Three Commonwealth Games Representatives
Three European Junior Representatives
Two National Championships
English National Schools Champions
Several Junior British National Records
Endless Numbers of Age Group Swimmers at National Level

Introduced:
Many U.S. Coaches to English Seminars, including Doc Counsilman and Don Gambril.

Foreword

It gives me great pleasure to write this for my good friend and colleague, George Bole. I have known George since 1967. It was he, while acting as secretary for the British Coaches Association, that first brought me to England, to present a lecture to that body in Leeds.

From that time on, George and I stayed in touch. I, along with so many others in the coaching fraternity, had a scare when George had a heart attack. Fortunately, as is George's way, he fought back and returned to the pool deck.

During his tenure in the United Kingdom, he produced many champions and national team members. His background of over forty years touched all levels of swimming. From teaching beginners, secondary school programs and age groupers to national level and international levels swimmers, all benefited from his personal interest, attention and techniques.

In 1984, George was invited to work in my camp in Alabama. It wasn't until he arrived, that he received his assignment. George was told he would be in charge of the Masters Section. Little did I know it would be the first step in a whole new world for George. He of course, did a marvelous job and was an instant hit with the Masters.

The rest of the story is still unfolding. He has had tremendous success with his St. Pete Club, doubling his numbers from 100 to 200, countless national champions in varying age groups, with substantial world records to complement these. Perhaps his crowning achievement was with the "Holmes Lumber Jax Team," in the 1988 World Masters Championship in Australia. They won 82 Gold Medals setting 52 world records, entering 189 swimmers to this meet.

The continued work George does, giving clinics and speeches, including the American Coaches Association, must qualify him for the title **"A Master Coach."**

Don Gambril
1984 U.S. Olympic Swim Coach

Preface

How to Use This Book

When George approached us in a quest to find a publisher for his material, he had certain elements he wanted the book to include. He wanted a small, handy book that could easily fit in a swim bag. He wanted something that the swimmers would use, and this meant allowing them to take his workouts to the pool and in the water. Furthermore, he wanted it affordable.

As we designed this book, our hope was to build a user-friendly package that engages readers. The most successful workout books convey the coach's personality, and you'll get to know Coach Bole as he makes several exceptional points in the opening chapters.

The drill chapter can keep variety in the workouts. Use them to spice up practices. The workouts in this book are tried and tested. This season was a huge success.

The first 85 workouts are built on two pages each with the dashed line to split the page in the middle. The left page, which is near the book's spine, is to remain in the book. The outside, which is on the right side, is to be cut or ripped from the book and taken to the pool.

With removable pages, you can take the practice to the pool, dunk it into the water, and then slap it on the wall near your lane. Or, you can put the wet workout on a kickboard, the starting block or inside a plastic envelope.

George says his swimmers often try to save wet practices to later insert in their a log books. Don't hesitate to write in this book. (Sorry librarians!) Note the date you swam the practice, changes, comments, etc. Let the remains of this book be your log.

Workouts 86-170 only appear once each, as we wanted to give the most bang for the buck, or pound.

Best of luck!

Publishers,
Swimming Support Syndicate

Chapter One

Tailoring Workouts for Masters

Most of the swimmers with pretensions to the highest honors attend one practice per day, although without any compulsion, some return to do more. As a coach, I like to monitor all their performances.

As my program is so well provided for, in terms of time and space, I do not have a set time for practice. I attend at the first light and supervise the early arrivals and stay for those who follow later. This involves a series of individual workouts tailored to individual needs. However, over the years, the swimmers wanting to swim as a group, have fitted themselves into like units and I have been glad to accommodate them accordingly.

It is from one of these groups, arriving regularly at 6:00 a.m., that I developed my daily workouts. This is a very enthusiastic, dedicated, diligent, forward-looking set of swimmers helping each other and themselves through their great application to the work set.

This group consists of competitors in the 50+, 40+, 30+ and occasionally younger age groups. All are capable of good solid performances and of averaging training rates of 3,000-3,500 yards per hour. This is my key group. Few, if any, were outstanding college or high school performers. Basically, they are the product of the Masters program. Their achievements include four All-American Awards, two World Records, three National Championships and a host of top ten USA places. Events covered were distances from 50 yards to 10,000 meters. Sufficient proof of efficient workouts?

Each day I select a workout tailored especially to the needs of this group, challenging them sufficiently to hold their interests. I use a great deal of variety of distances and strokes. I always have them wondering, "What's next?" The general yardage is from 4,000 to 4,750 yards according to the time of the year. This usually occupies one-and-a-half to two hours. Not all complete every workout, due to business commitments. Some have to leave the pool early.

Once this set is confirmed, I use the general theme of that workout for the rest of the team. Swimmers who are better than the key group will have increased distances with reduced take-off times to contend with. While the less capable will swim less distance with increased times. Many of those outside the key group require individual programs. But, where possible, all schedules follow a theme for the day.

Please do not take it that doing a written, prepared workout is the total answer to improvement. I am constantly scanning the pool for stroke defects, poor turns, indifferent drives off the walls, etc. If I consider it necessary, I may suspend the plan for some days to change the general tempo of the work being done, and when normalcy returns, it's back to the plan.

I cannot stress enough that lots of distance and effort without attention to good technique and efficiency is no substitute for good coaching. At regular times swimmers should endeavor to have their strokes examined to ensure that the energy expended is to their best advantage. A good coach can save thousands of yards through efficient advice. Be sure too, that the coach who advises you knows exactly what is wanted. Too many swimmers have been misled by badly informed "coaches."

While reading the included workouts, it will be noticed that almost all begin with a set warm-up of 500 yards. My reason for this, is that when the swimmers enter the pool they know to start the 500, giving me the time to place their workouts in their lanes. It saves time. But, I also like them to start competition warm-up similarly. Of course, the warm-up, as in all athletic endeavors, is very essential to later effort, loosening up the muscles and joints and easing up the heart rates.

It is also evident that I include a "warm down" of 200 or more yards at the end of each schedule. This is perhaps, sadly I'd say, the most neglected phase of swimming workouts or even competition. The warm down shortly performed allows the connecting tissues of the muscles to stretch and expand again after all the strain that they have suffered. Failure to warm down, causes soreness and stiffness the following day. All our swimmers warm down well after workouts and after every competitive swim. It is a worth while discipline easily learned.

There will be those who will wonder about a land conditioning program. Some of our people "do weights," but I do not have compulsory land conditioning. I know some do exercise with residence at various hospitals and health centers. I am aware of what they do and will advise if I think it necessary. I do have a few swimmers who believe in the efficiency of a weight program and for these, I use three morning sessions of around forty minutes. It is my contention if someone believes he/she needs such a program, then I should go along and help monitor it. But, with Masters having limited time due to business commitments, I would prefer them to spend the time in the pool. I think the best way to improve swimming is to swim.

While I confidently recommend these workout sessions, I would advise not to follow everything specifically. Swimming is perhaps the most individual of sports and each individual should examine what is asked of him/her and adjust and change if he/she thinks it necessary. Swimming is not yet a science, and like all art forms, is capable of many, many interpretations.

Chapter Two

Points to Ponder as you Paddle

Coaching on deck is like being a mirror for the swimmers. They cannot see what they are supposed to be doing, and trust that the coach will notice and feedback that information and corrections to them. So I feel that I am like some sort of video camera to play back pictures.

On the occasions when I see errors, I, like most interested coaches, often use pithy comments to make the pupils adopt corrections quickly. In this brief chapter I will try and give you examples of the types of reminders that may help you improve your technique. You have to imagine that I am instructing you alone and if you remember the most salient expressions then you will improve your technique. (I hope!)

Strokes

In FRONT CRAWL (freestyle is anything!) I often shout "make a hole in the water with your fingers" for your hands, wrists, elbows and shoulders to pass through. Watch your hands enter the water, good swimmers can see each hand enter in turn (good balance). Roll to breathe only when you see the wrist of the opposite hand enter the water, and return the head in time to see the recovering hand enter. This ensures good timing, eliminates early breathing and keeps the body on an even course.

Another popular phrase I use is "release the shoulder" (i.e., the opposite shoulder to help the distinctive roll necessary for good front crawl). Keep the elbows higher than the hands at all times in the stroke. Recover the hands, in a relaxed manner, as near to the surface of the water as possible in the interest of efficiency and economy of effort. Keep the stroke long and flowing, enter the fingers in front of the shoulder of that arm, and have them leave almost at the lower end of the thighs. Feel the water with the finger tips and hands, before using it (good catch and feel).

Keep the head position such as you can easily see the entry of the hands (i.e.. looking forward and down).

Now for BACKSTROKE: my favorite remark to backstrokers is "lie in the water, it is nice and soft, they make beds out of it." So I imply you should rest your shoulders on the water, not in it. Have the water touch around your chin (if you have more than one, the original!) and give your ear lobes a ride. As you swim, you should try and see the top of the plume of water made by your kicking. Eyes look at about 45 degrees to the horizontal.

An explicit description of the arm track is "Chop your ears off with your upper arms" as the hands enter. (Make for good entry position.) Keep arms straight in recovery, get little finger entry.

Roll the shoulders around the long axis of the body - head perfectly still. Try to look down the shoulder and arm before recovering the hand. This way the weight of the arm should be directly over the body and not outside of it causing dropping of shoulder and too-wide entry.

Again as in the front crawl, try to feel the water by having the palm of the hand against the water for the propulsive phase. Keep arm straight until it is in line with shoulder. From there shorten the lever - try bending the arm, keeping the elbow up. The stroke should flow and no hesitation is effected at the bottom of the push.

Legs should kick down fairly straight with a slight bend for the upward flick (like kicking a football). Please don't ride a bicycle kick on Backstroke, (i.e., bending knees on the downward beat). Remember to roll the hips in line with the shoulders. Practice kicking flutter on sides. Breathe in one arm, and out the other.

When I want to emphasize the shoulder roll and straight arm recovery, I'll yell "open up the side" (i.e., so that when the arm is at full extension the whole side of the body from toe to fingertip is exposed to view).

BREASTSTROKE: This is a stroke that is making strides; due, I think to the change in rules allowing the head to go underwater on each stroke.

Some poolside instructions are: Keep elbows in front of shoulders, at all times. Don't pause under the chest. Keep *sight* of hands always determining the width of the stroke. Try to keep the hands at angle of attack. They come together like a rooftop. This ensures the left force is maintained throughout all of the movement. The speed of movement of the hands should increase until full recovery position is reached. "Reach, Reach" is the cry for this operation.

For timing, as hands reach their widest points and start to press at the corners, the heels should begin to draw up - remember, the heels, not the knees, as in the wedge kick. Evert the feet and whip kick so the feet swirl like propeller blades with the ultimate touching of the big toes. Think of kicking the hands away.

As the hands go forward in the downward drive so should the head and upper body, causing the hips and legs to ride up on the surface. This is often referred to, in Europe, as the lunge breaststroke and was used by Adrian Moorhouse in equalling the World Record time for 100 meter Breast in 1:01.49! If you drive the feet down again - disaster! Disqualification

(D.Q.) for dolphin kicking - so draw them up as suggested.

The breath is taken late in the stroke when the arms are not quite fully open, and the out breath is as the face is in the water. Some good advice on breathing is "Don't come up to breathe, breathe when you come up."

There is little bend in the elbows in the modern breaststroke. Arms are almost straight throughout the out and down sweep and the in and up sweep.

Concentrate on the timing. Heels up as the hands press at the corners of the stroke.

FLY: Many people appear to take the title too literally - at least, it often seems to me. Seeing the great efforts some make to almost climb out of the water vertically, makes me want to award "WINGS." The butterfly movement refers to the wing span of the stroke, not its aerial power, the dolphin part is self explanatory.

Try to recover the arms easily and at full width, over the water. It is economic in energy terms to only just clear the water. I try to tell you to reach so your fingertips will touch the lane ropes. Remember recovery means just that, so don't waste energy by trying overly hard to throw the arms over. This often results in a great flop of hands on the water and then nothing. The work is to be done in and with the water, and not out of it.

I like you to keep low in the Fly - "breathe through your mouth not your stomach" is the cry. So try to keep the chin on the water as you breathe. Remember "breathe when you come up, don't come up to breathe." Recover arms in easy fashion, lead out with the elbows, then straighten the arms driving forward with the backs of the hands leading, thumbs down. Enter inside the shoulder width, stretch a little and scull before keyholing back with the hands. Speed the hand movements throughout the stroke exerting the greatest force at the final push through position. The fingers lead the hands out from the thighs for the easy recovery.

The breath is taken when the hands are directly below the shoulders. At this point the chin should be on the water to get the breath. Important pithy advice here is "Get your face back in the water before your hands enter, and get your face out before your hands leave the water".

Kick one is almost a reaction and happens as the entry is made. Kick two, major beat, is made as the hands are pushing through at the bottom of the stroke. Kick as though you were kicking from the neck down. Avoid excessive knee bending. Practice dolphin kick on your back to find the rhythm.

Turns

FRONT CRAWL: Increase pace as wall approach is made. Drop head and upper body as opposed to slowing down, raising the head and lifting the hips. Streamline the drive off the wall, hand over hand. Glide only sufficiently to hold speed of push. Turn and then twist not twist and turn.

BACK: Drop leading hand down the wall arching back and lowering head so as to facilitate pivoting around the lead hand and arm. Allow bending of the arm to use the momentum, raise hips and spin lower legs, arms stretch and feet push off from the wall streamlined. Don't use dolphin unless you are especially good at it.

For competitive swimmers who worry about the flags (and their heads), practice counting your strokes per length at sprint speed (50), at 100 speed and 200 speed, simulating competition conditions. This way, you won't have to trust flags or walls. The distances of the flags may vary but pool distances seldom do. A good turn at the right time can mean quite a savings and gain.

BREAST: Again, approach the wall at speed, trying to judge exactly where to drop at full stroke (only practice, practice and more practice will make it easy). Getting caught at half stroke (eating the wall) has made many a gold medal turn to silver or bronze. Short strokes if necessary should be judged before the wall stroke.

Keep the turn low and legal (again practice makes perfect). Rising high up the wall may look spectacular but is not economic. Judge the speed to the wall, don't glide too long, don't pull too soon.

Try to kick yourself to the surface so you are in full flight with no break in your movements. Do not confuse fast moving arms at the end of the breaststroke race, usually it means you are spinning your wheels. Keep your stroke at all times, extra speed means extra power - not turnover.

FLY: Like the breaststroke, good turns in Fly are best executed when the approach to the wall is at speed. And, as in the breaststroke, judging the exact distance for a full stroke turn is all important. Stroke counting helps. Unless you are extraordinarily proficient at dolphin then I should limit the number of kicks after the push off. I would advise no more than two.

After the start and turn of the Fly, try to take two strokes before a breath. Afterward breathe when you feel you need to. Champions from all times have had different breathing patterns. Develop what *suits you* and that with which you are comfortable. Sometimes when the hips and legs start to drag, breath holding for two or three strokes will redress the situation. Remember again, don't chop the strokes short to find speed, use the long stroke with technique and strength. The saying is "When you get tired think of your stroke."

To come back to mirroring the images from the pool, you may notice the coach use hand signals as he catches the swimmer's eyes.

If you should see me raise my elbow and tap it furiously, the message is that you are dropping your elbow or not recovering elbow first. At the signal I expect you to try and alter. Another time I will pat my forehead, trying to inform you to raise your head. If I should look like some crazy guy pushing one arm forward and then another it is likely you are swimming short or not rolling. Likewise, I may push my hands far behind me signalling that you are not finishing your stroke.

If, on Backstroke, you see me raise my arms up straight and close to my ears, that is exactly the message I wish to convey. Sometimes my hands will imitate a flutter kick - telling you to kick faster. The signals for shoulder rolling and hip rolling warrant little interpretation - but they are necessary to coach you in your techniques. Holding up the hand showing the little finger entry is also quite explicit.

Wide arms for breaststroke explain themselves. Heels up in hinge fashion indicate the kick is inadequate and needs adjusting. Head dropping is also clearly and easily conveyed. Indicating low forward position in the Fly is done by pressing the hands in a downward movement. Again width of the stroke is an easy matter to signal as is kicking faster.

There are also a lot of words I sometimes use from my selection of occupations and languages gathered on my travels. These I would not dare to put into print, not while the libel laws and the use of colorful description are still sacrosanct. Sometimes even words fail me - but still withal, I love all of you and the problems you pose.

P.S. These observations are my own - and are gathered from the archives of my ancient mind. If someone disagrees with my views, I don't mind, I am not claiming infallibility - even though I have kissed the floor many times for my views!

Chapter Three

Training and Coaching The I.M.

Perhaps the most exciting, interesting and, for the competitor, demanding event in the swimming program is the Individual Medley. With all four strokes involved and all five sources of energy used, training and coaching the medley is somewhat specialist in nature.

Yet for all its glamour and all the efficiency demanded for its execution, very little has appeared in any of the accepted tomes of swimming. Doc Councilman in *The Science of Swimming* (1986) devotes three chapters and two lines to pacing the I.M. plus five pages of training schedules out of 446 pages for our information on this "the most interesting of all competitive races." Derek Snelling, Canadian Olympic Coach from Calgary, wrote a book *All About Individual Medley* based on his own very wide experiences. Don Talbot, in his *Swimming to Win for All Ages* wrote one chapter, "So You Want to be a Medley Swimmer" and, incidentally, stated what I believe to be true, that the Backstroke leg is the strong point of the event.

More recently, Ernie Maglischo, in his wonderful book, *Swimming Faster* could only furnish us with three paragraphs on the I.M. and its training needs. In my research, I found one or two articles contributed to aspects of this event. So, all in all, it seems that little research has been done for the improvement of the I.M., or if it has been done extensively, then it's a well kept secret.

After the Montreal Olympics, I proceeded to attempt to analyze the results of the Medley (400), as the 200 was not swum then. My study was to find out and establish a percentage breakdown of the time spent on each stroke. Using both men's and women's splits for the finals, and averaging the percentage of the total time for each stroke, I arrived at the following conclusion. For all good Medleyists, 22.4% of the overall time was spent on butterfly, 25.5% on Backstroke, 29.5% on breaststroke, and 22.6% on Freestyle. The gold medalist for women, G.D.R.'s Ulricke Tauber split 22.5%, 25.3%, 29.2% and 22.9%, and Australia's Gail Neall won the Olympic 400 I.M. at Munich with a 22.6%, 25.6%, 29.7% and 22.2%. To add a topical note, Tomas Daruyi of Hungary in his 200 world record I.M. in Seoul returned figures to record 22.4%, 25.5%, 29.5%, and 22.6%.

So, now, to develop the I.M. swimmer's program, I am able to determine from an expected total time, how he/she should split his/her strokes. For instance, if I am hoping for a 5 minutes 00 seconds total time, then using the percentages, I want him or her to swim the following:
1 min 7.2 sec Fly, 1 min 16.5 sec Back, 1 min 28.5 sec Breast, and 1 min

7.8 sec Free. Now these figures are but guidance control, but from the analyses made, the swimmer should be near. At least, if he/she splits differently, he/she will have an idea where improvement should be made.

Medley swimming is one of the great conditioners in most successful coaches' programs. Bud McAlister, Janet Evan's coach, testifies to this as one of the reasons for his great protege's performances. Most of us use medley work, if only for variety, but I believe that to be successful in the event it must be treated as that, an event, in itself. It should not be treated as a potpourri of strokes, but as a complete entity, and so training for the I.M. must have that aspect in mind. From a survey I made of how the best British and European coaches approached the training for medley I had as many different schemes as individuals. Some used a different stroke each day, others combined two strokes per day, while many trained several days per stroke.

My own approach was, and still is, that if I am to treat the event as an entity then I must work on it that way. For instance, a complete medley workout could be:

WARM-UP :	100 FLY + 75 BK + 50 BR + 25 F/S 75 FLY + 50 BK + 25 BR + 100 F/S 50 FLY + 25 BK + 100 BR + 75 F/S 25 FLY + 100 BK + 75 BR + 50 F/S REST 10 SEC AFTER EACH 250
KICK :	4 X 75 I.M., 4 X 50 I.M., 4 X 25 I.M.
PULL :	8 X (4 X 25 I.M.) REST 10 SEC BETWEEN EACH OF THE 8 SETS
SWIM :	4 X 50 I.M. STRAIGHT + 4 X 50 I.M. REVERSED BREATHE 3 ON FLY, 4 ON BACK, EVERY 6 STROKES UNDERWATER FOR BREAST, AND EVERY 5 *BREATHING* FOR FREE (HYPOXIC)
SERIES :	4 X (4 X 50 I.M. + 50 FLY) 4 X (4 X 50 I.M. + 50 BK) 4 X (4 X 50 I.M. + 50 BR) 4 X (4 X 50 I.M. + 50 F/S)
SPRINT :	16 X 25 4 EACH STROKE EVERY SEC

There are infinite variations on this regimen, but sections of medley work should be a part of every workout. And the reason for working the event as a whole or with two or more strokes tied, is to familiarize the swimmer with the changes in body positions, and the need to tie-up the strokes.

From my questions to coaches as to the most important requirement for a medley swimmer, the most repeated answer was the "ability to tie the strokes together." My observations led me to believe that there is a question of balance involved in the changes from face down Fly, to upside down on Backstroke, change again to Breaststroke and face down again to Freestyle. After watching all over Europe and Great Britain, it was apparent that after completing each stroke swimmers tended to slow down for the first few strokes of the new leg. So the more often the swimmers accustom themselves to the changes the better would be their performances.

Further examination of the results of the world champion medleyists provided the interesting fact that the Freestyle legs compared favorably with the last 100's of the 400 Freestyle swimmers. This fact convinces me that good I.M.ers must have high endurance quality and so need some training for the middle distance Freestyle event.

Filip Dan, coach to many great Medleyists, made the point that he likes his swimmers to hit the Fly and Freestyle legs at similar times - bourne out by the percentage figures. To do so demands the performer to rate high on endurance.

If I want to improve one of the strokes in the medley, then, adhering to the theory that the event be treated as an entity, I would concentrate on the weak strokes within the context of the medley. In other words, to improve the Backstroke, I would swim sets of 25 Fly + 100 Bk + 25 Br, maintaining the prone-supine-prone formation. Similarly breaststroke would be 25 Back + 100 Br + 25 F/S, again keeping the pressure on the weakness and holding the body changes.

Pacing the I.M. is not easy for the uninitiated, but if we examine the energy sources used we might have some ideas. The start of the race, Fly, we see the energy coming largely from anaerobic sources for the first two minutes of the event. Lactic acid produced causes the lowering of the PH which is one of the stimulants of the increased respiration. Once respiration increases, aerobic energy sources become available and a steady state is reached. This is different for each swimmer. In this steady state of swimming, the performers usually try to save some anaerobic energy to bring it home.

Thus, the Fly leg utilizes 85% anaerobic energy , 15% on the Back (with effects of easier respiration), using 50% on the breaststroke becomes the steady state, 70%-30%, and the Freestyle, bringing it home, returns to the anaerobic sources. The importance of a really good Backstroke is obvious - most I.M.ers are outstanding on the dorsal event.

Our medley prospect would then be specific in his training all four strokes as much as possible, develop a good Backstroke, have a reasonably good 400 Freestyle with high endurance.

To swim the I.M. the best instruction I give is to swim the Fly knowing that there are three more legs to follow, push hard on the Backstroke, pull with wide arms on Breaststroke, using triceps to save the biceps for the Freestyle leg which should be a determined effort to round off the race.

Finally, if there is one weak stroke in the four, I would advise the competitor not to work that particular stroke too hard in the race. That results in a waste of useful energy needed to strengthen the effort on the other strokes. Swim the weak stroke with the best form possible and try to compensate on the good strokes.

Remember the percentages 22.4, 25.5, 29.5, 22.6 for the respective strokes, good turns to link up the event, middle distance pacing ability, a good Backstroke, and similar times for Fly and Freestyle. The rules are the same for age-group through Masters.

Chapter Four

Short Course Masters - A Season's Workouts

My motivation for this entire book was a desire to satisfy the many requests that I have received from Masters swimmers throughout the USA and abroad. Often these requests resulted in my spending a few workouts to try and help. So, I thought if I could supply a whole season's set of workouts such people would derive greater benefit.

It would appear that, despite being in existence more than twenty years, there is a great dearth of qualified sympathetic Masters coaches serving the 30,000 plus Masters swimmers in the USA. I have noticed at the Masters National and International meets few coaches were on deck and in conversation with many of the entrants, I discovered that the greatest complaint was lack of coaching and direction.

So, bearing in mind that at my own program, St. Petersburg Masters, has been instrumental in developing World record breaking performances, National champions, and Regional winners of all ages at all distances, I assumed that what they did in their workouts for a season would commend itself. In 1989, St. Pete Masters Award Committee honored twelve All-Americans, six National Champions, three World Record Breakers (eight

W.R.s between them) and numerous Top Ten Honorees. I believe what these people did in preparation for these results is worthy of emulation.

I would be remiss not to make mention of Ray Burns who has carefully collected and catalogued every workout I have given him for the past six seasons. Indeed, it is mostly at his suggestion that this book has been written.

The following is how I look at my season. I use three peaks at which to point my program. The first important occasion is the One Hour Swim in January. This event enables me to direct the swimmers to build up lots of yardage for the oncoming competitive season.

From October until January, each year my workouts are based on developing pace swimming - the pace being that at which is required to attain a good distance for the hour swim. I determine what each swimmer should achieve, distance-wise, and then set the pace accordingly. Thus, all preparation for the October to January period sacrifices speedwork so that the necessary pace is established, (i.e. short-rest work at no more than 90% effort). I know this approach works because each year St. Pete Masters score high in this One Hour Swim event.

The second peak for my season is the St. Pete Regional Championships. This is a very prestigious, well-attended meet, which claims to be the largest running meet (20 years) in Masters swimming. This takes place around the end of March or beginning of April.

Following the Hour Swim, I examine the specified events favored by each swimmer. I introduce a little more speed with lengthening rests and pay close attention to specific strokes and distances. The swimmers are alerted to what sort of times they need to improve personally, to score on top ten performances, and to achieve National Championship medal standards.

For those going on to the Nationals, usually three or four weeks later, I devise special preparations and workouts to help them recover from the Regionals and re-psyche for the Big One.

After Short Course Nationals, St. Pete Masters go long course to prepare for Long Course Regionals, Long Course Nationals, and the 10K swim. Preparations for these events may be the subject of another book, but for now let us consider the short course season. I must stress that none of our many successes has been accomplished without much blood, sweat, and yes, tears.

Our pool in St. Petersburg is one of the most beautifully appointed facilities for training in the world. A 50 meter x 25 yard open air tank is fronted by silver beaches, palm trees and the lovely Tampa Bay. Bathed in the glorious, golden sunshine of Florida this excellent facility is the Leisure Department's contribution to aquatics.

The Masters work out every morning from 6:00 a.m. until 9:00 a.m. and every afternoon from 4:30 p.m. until 6:30 p.m. Monday thru Friday. They rest Saturdays and have Sunday morning practices from 9:30 to 12:30 p.m.

Once a month there is a Masters Developmental Meet with a limited number of events.

Chapter Five
Fear

Its Importance--and the Answers in Masters Swimming

Fearfully, I dare to open this paper with the oft-repeated, still very much true cliche, "There's nothing to fear but fear itself." I will elaborate on these words as I proceed.

During my three years as coach to St. Petersburg Masters swimmers, I have garnered a lengthy list of apprehensive approaches towards the various aspects of the program.

To begin with, prospective members, after much heart-searching, usually come to see me with unnecessarily tentative approaches. Often, ladies with three children in an Age-Group program nearby, bashful to an extreme, confess the fear that "after all these years" they would or might look less than Sylvian in a swimsuit and wonder if I have any reasonable answer or cure that would help to persuade them to overcome the fear. Men, too, express similar "fear" -- often patting their waistlines to indicate their self-consciousness.

To such applicants, let me assure them that their "shapes," "forms," "figures"--or whatever--matter not one whit to the others on the team. First, most of their peers have experienced exactly what they are going through, and are more than willing to be supportive of them. They will delight in telling the new-comers how they dealt with the problem. Second, I can assure you that those in my programs will be too busy with the work in hand to spend time studying your "form."

Next, I meet the softly-spoken, timid people who are "not very good swimmers," who are afraid that by joining Masters they will be "made to take part" in competition. They just want to improve the strokes and swim laps at the times the program operates.

For these people, and their fears, let me say that the only demand--no!--request, made to new masters is that they might come along and help at a competition at our pool. We are always short of helpers to time, count, help with hospitality, etc. No one demands actual swimming participation from them. And as to their self-confessed lack of ability, everyone on the team is "not so good." The term is relative. There are some better than others, but in Masters who cares? The coach cares, and it is his job to help you feel better in the water. You will improve as all the others in the pool have improved. Again, your new friends will offer you advice ad nauseum. You need never fear feeling inadequate. The program is constructed so as to help you. If you need special advice, please feel free to ask. I love helping people swim well.

Now, we have those who used to swim in high school, college. . . but have been out of it so long that they fear they may be so much "out of shape" that they will either "look ridiculous" or hold the program back. Getting in shape is no problem for the person who has had some background in a competitive program of training. Getting in shape in a couple of weeks is quite a different problem! To get back to those high school times requires patiently building up your degree of fitness, and this can be done for you. Indeed, several of our members boast of swimming times better than those of their high school days! Dispel that fear as to looking ridiculous, I can assure you that after almost four decades pounding a pool deck, that swimmers working out are seldom aware of anything other than the clock, the lines on the pool bottom, the Backstroke flags and the pool ends. Occasionally they notice the coach! Other people's conditions do not come to their notice. Again, I will delight in coaching you stroke-wise.

I almost forgot the swimmers who join "for exercise only" and who would like to do "Freestyle" or "butterfly" properly but aren't interested in racing. No coach worth his salt would want anyone competing who doesn't want to race. But this coach, as someone with an aesthetic sense for the art of coordinated propulsion (Sea World) through the water, will want you to swim more easily, more proficiently and more elegantly. So I will endeavor to allay any fears about your ability to swim like the stars, teach you the newest techniques and make you happily more proficient. And then maybe with your new-found skills you might be tempted to try an odd team race or an individual, fifty-yard event. Besides, with this new proficiency you will be able to exercise more for the same outlay of energy.

The "health hazard syndrome" is another problem I confront often. Now let me state from the outset, that I, as a very ordinary guy, sans medical training or knowledge, am loath to say that swimming will improve whatever may be ailing you. I do know that people who swim regularly in my program certainly feel better. I believe that's because swimming is such a great sport and done properly makes people happier. This in turn will have advantageous effects for them physically. But, I feel that anyone with doubts about their physical conditions should consult their doctor before joining the program, and then, in confidence, tell the coach. This way there need be no fear of workouts causing physical aggravation or complaints. Remember that Masters programs throughout the world are thronged with people who have joined because they have health problems. Many Masters--recipients of heart by-pass operations--take part in regular swimming workouts and competitions. Similarly, asthma and chest sufferers comprise many of our ever growing number. And they are enjoying the opportunities of taking part. So fear no more--get in the swim!

For those fearful of not being able to "keep up," there need be little apprehension. "Keeping up" is not an expression used in Masters Swimming. We don't have people with whom one is required to "keep up." Each swimmer competes with himself. To start with, you will work at improving your own standards. The coach should--and in my case, will--map out your progression and as you advance you will be aware of your own improvement. Talk to those around you--they will relate their experiences--much like your own you'll find. So, fear of not keeping up is dead.

Finally, in this section for aspiring Masters, I meet the entrant who fears--how he/she fears! --that to swim Masters necessitates two-a-day, two hour sessions of 6,000 yards a piece, getting into the pool at 6:00 each morning and returning again each evening swimming until 9:00 p.m. I have news for such terrified prospective members--our program operates as such: morning training begins at 6:00 a.m. (I told you so, I hear) and usually ends at about 8:40 a.m. That doesn't mean that you must attend and be on the deck ready to go at 6:00 a.m. and work through until you're water-logged. Because many of our team go to work early and aren't done in time for the 4:30 p.m. evening session, we are allowed--with the good grace of the Leisure

Department--to start at 6:00 a.m. If you wish to come at 6:30, 7:00, 7:30, as many do, I will be there and I 'll direct your workout. If you are not a "morning person"--a lovely Americanism--then you may attend between 4:30 and 6:30 p.m. You may swim the whole session or any part of it--it's up to you. Sunday mornings you may come from 9:30 until 12:30 p.m.--or any part of that time. You please yourself. So be not afraid that you are going to give your whole life to swimming.

Competitive Masters and Their Fears

Over my many years in this wonderful sport, I have experienced and witnessed the ice-cold, dreaded hand of fear on the competitive swimmer. It has been responsible for the losses of titles, championships, fond hopes and aspirations. Now I find that fear still plays a very prominent part in the performances at the Masters level, too, so maybe it might be interesting to examine where fear lurks.

Naturally, the very first fear for competitors is of taking part. To be the cynosure of all eyes as one climbs up on the block is terror enough, but there is the added fear of looking ridiculous (at my age!). Everyone is looking at you. Nonsense, don't even turn one hair, because I can assure you, disconcerting as it may be, that outside of your immediate supporters and your competition, no one even notices you. In less than a couple of minutes or so, no one will even recall your swim (sometimes even the timer forgets!)

Another fear, self-imposed, is that of insufficiently working equipment. Goggles that slip off, cloud up, leak, etc. Hats too tight or too loose with the accompanying discomfort. Suits with untied strings, with straps that rub or are too baggy causing drag. Starting blocks that are shaky. These fears can be dispelled and should be by the competitor. All equipment should be tried out in warm-up prior to the competition.

Heat-sheets often create fear in many competitors. I've watched people feverishly going through the sheet to see who the competition is and which heat they're in and what time submitted. Always I hear that everyone (who hasn't "sandbagged") has a better time. The fear reduces some people to miniscule size. And it shouldn't! If you are prepared for the event and you are aware of what to expect then fear no one but yourself because that's who you are in competition with. Swim for your own improvement. If you have done everything you should to get a result, then have no fear. You will swim your best.

Of course, the competitor who has all sorts of gripes about his/her lane placement is also displaying a bad case of nerves--fear. He/she hates the outside lane because of the wash, etc. or hates the pole position in the middle because he/she is expected to be the fastest. Or the same competitor hates to swim next to a certain other person. Such competitors are usually fearsome of losing, and are usually preparing a whole set of excuses for losing. He/she can't accept the blame for not winning (if "blame" there ever is). To these people, I'd say, it doesn't matter at all, the world won't stop if you don't win and if you do your very 100% best, then whatever happens you can't lose. In Masters swimming there are no losers. There are others who may be faster, but everyone who takes part and tries honestly is a winner.

Another group familiar to the fear syndrome are those often conscientious folk who feel that either they have not done enough preparation or have done too much. These people worry too if they have tapered too long or not long enough. To such people, I would say, get a reputable, knowledgeable coach and let him accept the responsibility and fear that goes with it. And I can assure you that coaches at all levels--from Olympic to Age Group--suffer monumental fears on account of adequacy or other aspects of tapering.

If you haven't a coach, I would advise you to keep a log book and check back on previous preparations. This way you will see when you had your best performances and what you did beforehand. This would be your taper and if you are satisfied, then fear goes through the window.

We come now to a whole series of recognizable fears and--I hope--cures for them. One that stands out a lot is the fear of swimming the race in the wrong manner. That is, the swimmer who is afraid of going out too fast lest he may not finish! This baffles me, we have competitors training 5,000 to 7,000 yards per day and yet are scared they won't finish 200 yards. Usually these people, to coin a Braininism, want to "arrive alive" and do so with an explosive twenty yards after the opposition has finished.

The obvious cure for this type of swimmer is to pace their efforts in warmup. Know your pace for coming home and practice it. Once you repeat this four or five times with reasonable rests, you can stop worrying and get on with doing well in the competition.

The following fears will only be dispelled by assiduous practice:

1) the fear of false-starting,

2) of being left on the block,

3) of disqualification for stroke, turns and finishes, or

4) fear of take-overs in team race situations.

Only daily practice will make you feel really confident on these points. If you work at them, you should anticipate--not fear--the occasions.

Finally, there are other little personal fears that harm some of our more sensitive members. There is the obvious one--fear of being the slowest--of being *last*. To this I would say that one may be last in the race, but try and remember there are hundreds of thousands of people your age who would be far behind you. You are the last of an elite group. Chin up--no fear.

Chapter Six
Drill for Skill

Editor's Note: The following chapter is excerpted from *Drill for Skill for Swimming* written by George Bole and commissioned by the Executive Committee of the British Swimming Coaches' Association and Arena. The book was devised as a compilation of skill-drills to develop strokes, starts, turns and the I.M. *Drill for Skill for Swimming* was originally published in 1986.

As most swimming teachers and coaches are very much aware, the individual variance in styles of swimming are legion, depending on the physical and mental qualities of the swimmer. But, the performance of the individual age-group swimmer relates directly to his mastery of essential swimming skills. Doc Counsilman's *Science of Swimming* has observed that "great swimmers never seriously violate basic mechanical principles, whilst poor swimmers almost always do." It is, therefore, the task of the advanced teacher or coach to assume the attainment and development of proper stroke mechanics by his squad or group.

The problem for the coach is to design the teaching methods best suited for him to help develop the improvement. The commonly accepted ways of either initial stroke instruction or subsequent stroke correction are the part-whole, the whole, and the progressive-part methods. Again Counsilman, in *Science of Swimming* states, "the method of teaching a skill should be dependent upon the complexity of the skill and the motor educatability of the learner. In learning simple skills, the whole method is superior to the other two. In learning more complex skills, the part-whole method and the progressive-part method are superior to the whole."

Stroke correction is of primary importance, once the basic skills are mastered. Continual effort must be made to acquire all the fine movements necessary to achieve the correct stroke. The initial stage of correction is the isolation of the stroke component in question. Part learning drills of kicking, pulling, single arm pulling are valuable techniques which allow the swimmer to focus attention on movements over which previously he had little control.

When using drills for stroke correction, it should be remembered that children have more difficulty than adults in balancing the difference between speed and accuracy of movement. In order to master a more intricate stroke movement, the swimmer will have to sacrifice speed initially. In fact, the coach should have his charges over-learn accuracy, for in daily workouts the whole process will be reversed, that is, the accuracy will lessen with practice as speed increases. But, the object of the exercise, is to produce accuracy and speed, if the coach is to develop a skilled swimmer. So it is, that the coach should keep the swimmer holding accurate movements while gradually increasing speed until his goal is reached.

In the competitive swimming situations familiar to most coaches there are usually a number of swimmers competing for limited pool space, and for the coaches' attention. Because of the limitations, it is impossible to conduct a one-to-one coach/swimmer instruction program. So the use of skill drills within the training workout is a practical and efficient method of correcting and improving strokes. The programmed workout does not suffer nor stop for the instruction, and in my experience is often enriched because of it.

A skill drill is the stroke or turn broken down into parts - usually parts that are weak. Often the skill drill will be an over-exaggeration - used often in early season 5 or 10 minutes during the workout in the heavy training season. These drills can be used very seriously during the taper period in an attempt to sharpen up the strokes, turns and approach to the wall, etc. They may also be used as part of a warm-up, workouts or a race. Also for a few minutes as active rest, and as a corrective measure for sloppy turns - between series.

Various skill drills can be worked into the regular training routine once the skill drill has been learned correctly. Howard Friby, World-known Canadian Coach and Author, talked about this feature in his presentation at the Montreal American Swim-Coaches Association Clinic. An example would be 10 x 100 of stroke building crawl, given set rest or send-off time. Use right arm only going up the pool, left coming back, two right, two left, the third 25 and four right, four left, coming home. Obviously there are many variations and combinations, the coach can use in this series, according to the needs of his swimmers.

Almost any aspect of technique can be implanted by the use of intelligent stroke drills, be it arm entry, kicking, breathing, turning or co-ordination. Remember, to teach the pupils the purpose of the drill to be used. "Nothing is learned until it is taught." Good swimmers make complex movements look simple because of their efficient performance of the techniques involved. That passage from simplicity to complexity and back to simplicity demands that all the parts should be practiced separately, then put together emerging in an efficient, simple-looking stroke, demonstrating speed and grace.

In outlining and researching the skill drills included, I have been motivated from watching Age-Group Championships particularly, the eleven year olds. These are the top groups in the country according to times standards, yet when one looked beyond the top few, the technical performance was lacking a great deal. I feel that this situation may have developed because of the size of the large training schemes and the difficulties of the coaches to coach-in-individual skill. Perhaps the use of these drills might help to improve the situation until swimming has produced more coaches.

Front Crawl

Skill Drills:

It is within the scheme of things, that most work done in training squads is on front crawl for the obvious reasons, of time, conditioning, space in lanes, etc., so it is with front crawl that we start our drills.

Front Crawl Kicking Drills:

1. Kick front crawl using kick board, head raised. (General conditioning exercise).

2. Kick front crawl using kick board with arms outstretched and face in water, breathing on every sixth kick. (Improves streamlining and VO_2 capacity).

3. Kick with arms extended, hands overlapped, face down between arms, breathe to the front on sixth kick.

4. As 3, but with head raised to improve power of kick.

5. Kick front crawl - arms at sides - face in water breathe to alternate sides every 6th kick.

6. As in 5 but with head up - to improve power of kick.

7. Kick - arms extended - under water (feeling use of all of the leg in the kick) (quick breaths and submerge).

8. As in 7 but with hands at sides.

9. Kick on right side, left hand spearing in front, right side of face resting on right shoulder, left hand at side and back straight.

10. Kick on left side, side of face resting on left shoulder, right hand at side - back straight.

Drills 9 and 10 will help to check the amplitude between knees in the kick.

11. Kick front crawl on right side as in drill 9 for 12 kicks then change to left side for 12 and so on. Ensure that body keeps streamlined position throughout the change and face rolls through the water.

12. Vary drill 11 by reducing number of kicks to six before change and then to three. (Will help breathing position).

The following are drills used by some of the better squads I've visited during 1982:

(a) Kicking silent front crawl using two or three kick boards on top of each other, feet below surface.
(b) Kicking exaggerated front crawl with feet high out of the water - one kick board - strengthening.
(c) Kicking front crawl with hands clasped behind back and chin on surface of water - strengthening and conditioning.
(d) Kicking front crawl using fins - obviously to help ankle flexibility.

Within a workout, one could use several variations of these drills to help the squad kick (i.e., 25 on side, 25 head up, 25 other side, 25 head down).

As one coach put it to his squad, "kicking is important. All the big muscles are in the legs and these are farthest away from the heart."

Front Crawl Arms Drills

1. Chicken wing drill: swimmers put thumbs in armpits, kick front crawl down the pool, breathing every 3, and stroking with the "chicken wings."

Not too much time should be spent on this drill. Coaches should only use it to sell the high elbow action and the rotation of the shoulders to aid recovery.

2. Start out a few strokes on "chicken wing" then start to push the forearm and hands forward to entry position: (high elbow and hand drag).

3. Begin as in drill 2, but push water forward with backs of hands, so that swimmer recovers with high elbow and drags hand through the water.

4. Start as in 3, but instruct swimmers to clear fingernails over the surface from leaving water to entering. (Aids relaxed and low recovery of arms).

5. Swim 100 yards - 25 chicken wing, 25 with hands pausing at armpits before entry, 25 with hands pushing water forward and 25 clearing fingernails.

I've found this series helps the younger swimmers to develop a compact style of crawl, having high elbow recovery, with hands low and close to body width. It is useful to obviate the lateral arm sweepers.

6. Swim one length (with high elbow, etc. as from previous sets of drills) using fists, emphasizing pulling with forearms (helps bend of arm).

7. Swim one length fists, opening hands after pull, to push back to thighs (for push part of stroke).

8. Swim one length full stroke, emphasizing the value of hands as paddles.

The use of fist swimming is used by many leading coaches to:

(a) develop the power phase being executed in a straight line.
(b) to correct the glide away of hands after entry.
(c) to ensure the stroke is not performed too far away from the body.
(d) to stop the hand trailing the elbow.
(e) to prevent an arm recovery that may be too wide and flat.

For the ordinary arms conditioning drills, where the arms are to be isolated in the stroke, the following drills are standard practice in most modern programs.

9. Swim arms only front crawl with legs apart and drifting.

10. Swim arms only with pull-buoys and using bands around ankles. (Care must be taken that body position is not too far off horizontal).

11. Swim arms only with pull buoys.

12. Swim arms only using only band or tube.

13. Swim using paddles, pull buoys and bands.

14. Swim using paddles, and pullbuoys.

15. Swim using paddles, legs trailing.

I have often used just the one paddle at a time if I needed to correct a particularly outstanding error in pulling technique in the particular hand movement.

Combinations of arms and kicking drills are used to help develop coordination within the stroke, helping breathing and all the time useful for correction and improvement of technique.

If we refer back to the kicking practice where the swimmer lay on his side with one arm extended and kicked on his side, we can develop a series of drills to introduce the arms into the stroke which help to improve coordination within the stroke.

16. Kick a length of the pool with right arm extended, head resting on right shoulder, left arm by side.

17. Repeat on opposite side.

18. Starting position as in drill 16, count 10 kicks, press water with right hand and at the same time lift the left elbow to recovery position. While the right hand is pulling through, the left continues to recover, as the body rolls through the water, face down, to the opposite side. As the right arm finishes the push phase the left hand enters the water.

19. Same as 18 starting on left side.

When the roll-through and correct stroke pattern are mastered using ten kicks, then the count drops to six and finally to three on each side. A special reminder must be given to make sure the legs continue the kick while rolling through from one position to other.

20. With right arm extended use left arm, having left hand touch right at entry. (Helps to lengthen stroke, keeps elbow up and brings entry hand towards central axis position).

21. As in drill 20, but instruct swimmers to take breath as left hand approaches thighs and return face to water before it touches right hand.

22. With left arm extended use right arm as drill 20.

23. Again reverse arms and continue as drill 21.

24. Use left arm, keeping left shoulder against the wall, with right hand out in front.

This drill stops lateral swing and avoids pulling hand straying outside body line. Insist on swimmer keeping elbow high and hand low in recovery phase.

25. As 24 using right arm.

26. Swim front crawl with head raised watching entry of hands. (Strengthens arms, improves entry position and assists high elbow recovery).
27. Swim front crawl face on water, watching for paths of thumbs through the water (useful for improving bend in arms and to stop the very deep reaching especially on non-breathing side).

28. Swim front crawl as 27, but insist on touching thighs with thumbs before recovery. (Keeps stroke long).

29. Swim front crawl, directing swimmers to try to brush ears with shoulders (Assists flexibility of shoulders in stroke).

30. Swim front crawl, exaggerating roll of body, keeping head aligned all the time with the body, so that swimmer rolls enough to clear mouth for breath. (Helps to clear shoulders, and to use opposite shoulder in pull).

31. Swim front crawl, trying to put into practice the points practiced in the session.

Other drills that I've either used, seen or read about are:

32. Swim front crawl, hesitating recovery at arm pit, before entry. (Improves the high elbow position, strengthens kick and assists a cleaner entry).

33. Catch-up front crawl used by some coaches to improve alignment and to lengthen stroke. Swimmer pushes off with both hands and arms extended, then pulls with right arm (or left), through the movement, stopping on surface on contact with left hand (or right), which then operates as opposite hand did previously. Thus the swimmer continues. (Many coaches doubt the side-effect of this drill, which can cause a slide and glide type of stroke).

34. A drill of Cecil Colwin's to cure the slide and glide swimmer is to have the swimmer extend one arm **out** of the water while the opposite arm strokes continuously.

35. All or almost all of these drills may be further developed using a paddle or paddles.

Back Crawl

British Swimming has been weakest in back crawl for more than a decade. Perhaps the best known performers, on the dorsal stroke, relative to Europe and the World, have been John Brockway, Graham Sykes among the men and Judy Grinham, Margaret Edwards and Natalie Steward among the women, and those days are long gone now.

On examination, this stroke is not nearly so popular as are the other strokes, partly I suspect because lying on one's back, groping for unknown water and pushing forward to go backward does not sound the most attractive of propositions. I feel also that with the advent of the larger squads, there is a lot less opportunity for the Backstroke swimmer to do specific work - plus the preponderance of circle swimming necessary to accommodate the bigger numbers makes life extremely difficult for the youngster with aspirations to being a Backstroke expert.

However, as anyone, who has had the privilege to have watched Roland Matthes swim, will attest, the stroke, when performed properly is a joy to behold. Before beginning to drill the squad it would certainly be helpful to use a video of a good backstroker, so the fluency of the stroke may be seen, and the aims of the exercise stated.

Back Crawl Kicking Drills:

1. Kick, arms at sides, (emphasize - toes just to break surface - "make water boil").

2. Kick, hands on thighs, head forward enough for swimmer to see top of splash made by feet.

3. Using a lightly weighted tube (12" x 1½" diameter) held in front of hips. Kick back crawl (assists natural swim position and stops back arching).

4. Holding kick board beneath head, kick Backstroke (use board as pillow).

5. Extend arms, holding kick board behind head, kick back crawl (strengthens kick and improves body alignment).

6. As drill 5 but without kick board.

7. Clasp hands and extend arms behind head, trying to rest head on upper arms (improves body alignment and head position).

8. Using weighted tube (see drill 3) hold tube at ends, extend arms beyond head and kick Backstroke. (Improves flexibility of shoulder, holds hands below surface of water and overloads the kick).

9. With hands at sides, kick back crawl and after six kicks raise right arm with elbow locked to 45° with horizontal - continue for length.

10. As in drill 9 but use left arm.

11. Start as in drill 9 but alternate raising and lowering of arms every six kicks. Proceed to three kicks (improves the strength of kick and introduces the straight arm ready for recovery).

12. Push off on back and raise both arms to 45° to horizontal and further kick (over loads kick strengthens quadriceps).

13. Kick back crawl, hands at sides, roll on to right side raising left shoulder and elbow clear of the water for six kicks, change to left side raising right shoulder and elbow clear - proceed in stages to three kicks per side (introduces longitudinal rolling of the body in the stroke and promotes the practice of clearing shoulder before recovery of arm begins).

14. Flutter kick on right side, hands at sides, (waving legs from hips - keep back straight).

15. As drill 14, but on left side. (These drills familiarize swimmers with water pressure on whole leg during kick).

Back Crawl Arms Drills:

1. With right arm extended, left arm at side, flutter kick on side.

2. With left arm extended, right arm at side, flutter kick on side.

3. Start as in drill 1 and after ten kicks, pull strongly with right hand and arm rolling across back to the other side recovering left arm and reaching to full extension in front.

4. Proceed in stages from ten kicks to six kicks to three kicks. (These drills assist coordination and teach swimmers on Backstroke to pivot the shoulders in position for recovery).

5. Swim 200 to 400 using this method concentrating on the straight arm recovery, the lift of the shoulder, the roll into the pull and the pivoting of the shoulders on the axis formed by the **still head** and spinal column.

6. Don Gambril, U.S.A. Olympic coach and coach of Alabama University uses the following four practices to develop the bent-arm pull:

(a) Stand on the bottom at shallow end, arms extended downward at the sides about 12" from each thigh, thumbs pointing outward palms towards the shallow end wall. Push water with each hand alternately. As the water is pushed toward the shallow end, the fore arm rotates inward and the wrist snaps so the palm ends up facing away from the shallow end. This action simulates the final push phase of the arm pull.

(b) Kick down the pool on back, arms extended toward the feet and start alternate action of the hands, rotating the forearm toward the body and pushing water with the hands. Make sure the swimmer's thumbs are coming up and over on the push phase.

(c) With the left arm held in the water at an extended position over the head at the catch position kick and swim a length using right arm only and concentrate on the pattern of the movements of drills (a) and (b).

(d) Extend the right arm at the catch position over the head and kicking on back swim with the left arm.

7. A further development of the drills to establish the push phase of the Backstroke is to swim double-arm Backstroke, (i.e., start with arms extended overhead, kick Backstroke and then pull with both arms to side, and continue for length of pool).

8. Arms extended, kick Backstroke then push water through, along sides with palms at right angles. Recover arms with backs of hands together and do not start pull until hands are under water.

Have swimmers notice the movement of the body when the push is made. This exercise also is good for shoulder mobility.

9. Swim 25 right arm, 25 double arm, 25 left arm, 25 double arm for 400 yards.

10. Using right arm only (back crawl) raising and rolling left shoulder back to develop shoulder raise rhythm in stroke.

11. As in drill 10 opposite swim and shoulder.

12. Single arm back crawl, but make a quarter arm recovery (non-stroking arm) and raise shoulder of recovery arm.

13. Single arm back crawl, but make a half arm recovery.

14. Single arm swims. Develop from drills 12 and 13 for a few strokes until going into the full arm recovery. (Assists development of full stroking rhythm with shoulder lift in recovery).

15. Using variations of one arm swimming as, 3 right, 3 left, 3 full stroke, 3 right 1 left, 2 right 1 left, etc.

16. Use catch-up drill as, start back flutter kick with arms extended beyond head, pull one arm through stroke and back to extended non stroking hand, which upon touch will stroke. (Assists flexibility and location of entry behind head).

From experience catch-up drill may also develop the bad habit of stopping the stroking hand at water surface behind the head. To counter act this danger I use the following drill.

17. Back flutter kick, hands at sides, after six kicks, recover right arm and hand through the Backstroke path back to side, whereupon the left arm will act.

18. Speed up this drill cutting down the delay at the legs (accentuate the direct entry of the hands in the catch position).

19. A further drill for developing the direct entry is to use the fists.

20. Using fist drill for entry then opening hand for push will develop "feel" of the water in push phase.

21. Most of the drills may be performed using the usual aids.

22. Arms only drill using pull buoy.

23. Arms only with leg band around ankles (increases resistance).

24. Arms only with rubber band around ankles (further increases resistance).

25. Using paddles, pulling Backstroke.

26. Add pull buoys to drill 25.

27. Further add rubber band around ankles (all increasing resistance).

28. Use paddle on one hand only, pulling Backstroke and kicking (to improve strength of paddle arm and hand in stroke).

29. Use weighted wrist-bands and pull Backstroke (strength and assists direct entry into catch).

I believe that it is not advisable to have the youngest age groups using paddles in Backstroke. From medical sources it would appear that there is a danger of severe shoulder joint problems developing.

As in the front crawl, combinations of these drills can be used within a workout. They can be utilized for parts of warm-up practice, and for stroke sharpening during the delicate taper stage.

Starts and Turning Drills for Back Crawl:

For the Backstroke start, the important practice is the push-off on the back.

1. Practice across pool. Place feet on wall about hip width apart, push with hands at sides (measure distance).

2. As in drill 1 but this time stretch arms to full extension with hands touching as push is executed (measure distance).

3. As in drill 2 but insist on full ankle extension to arrive at most streamlined position.

4. Repeat practice 3 but have swimmer drop feet lower on wall so he/she pushes off from a deeper position.

5. As drill 4 plus complete the width by introducing flutter kick.

6. With feet in stagger position on wall, hands gripping bar at shoulder width, practice throwing the arms laterally to have hands touch at full arms extension.

7. As above but have swimmer bring head forward as arms go back (preventing deep entry and slowing of start).

8. As 7 plus introduction of leg kick as speed slackens.

9. As 8 plus one arm pull. Emphasize that this is the most important stroke in the swim. It is the stroke that launches the body into speed.

10. To facilitate the clearing of the hips over the water at the start, have a lane rope about one meter back from start and have swimmers practice clearing it each time.

Back Crawl Turns:

I have found this aspect of Backstroke has been very much neglected in teaching and coaching. Most of our swimmers drift into Backstroke turning. Very few teachers or coaches seem keen to work on Backstroke turning practice. Perhaps with better application to turning, our woeful standards in Backstroke events might improve.

1. Swimmers lie on back, keeping head on surface, raise knees up so heels are touching seat and then spin round using hands and arms to rotate against the water.

2. As in drill 1 but execute turns to 180°.

3. As in drill 2 except that swimmer starts from supine outstretched position legs should be tucked up very fast with the lower legs describing a semi-circle over the surface in the movement.

4. Have the swimmers start from end of bath on Backstroke and swim fifteen yards at speed executing drill 3 to return to starting end. (Insist on speed of movement at turning point).

5. From half way mark, swimmer will swim Backstroke at speed until close to the bath end and execute turn just before he touches wall, then he stretches out to push off in the opposite direction.

These practices are to have the swimmer acquire the body twists involved in turning:

6. Swimmers stand about five yards out from bath-end. On their backs, they kick in to wall, with right arm and hand extended until hand contacts wall with fingers pointing down (the contact must be made below surface) and

they execute the turn as practiced in drills 4 and 5.

7. As practice 6 but work on the vigorous push-off in streamlined position from wall.

Remind swimmers that if feet touch high on wall then push will be to the bottom of pool with subsequent loss of time and speed.

8. Practices 6 and 7 should now be done using the left hand.

At this stage, I find it important that backstrokers learn to turn on either hand and do not develop a "wrong hand."

9. It is good practice to count strokes from flags to wall so that the swimmer does not have to spend so much time and speed looking for the wall. This stroke counting should be done at racing speeds, otherwise the whole thing could go very wrong in a competition.

10. Swimming across the pool, have the swimmers count the strokes and turning without looking for the wall. (Helps swimmer lose fear of wall and usually assists in turning on either hand.)

11. From drill 10 have the swimmers on lengths counting the strokes from time the head passes the flags.

A very nice exercise that will interest backstrokers is to swim as far as possible with a half filled beaker of water balanced on forehead. (This drill will help stabilize head position).

Butterfly

The butterfly stroke is the second fastest used in competition, giving way only to front crawl, but only marginally. Officially it has only been accepted for competition since the 1952 Olympics. The world record time for 100 meters Fly held by American Bill Paulus is 53.81 sec and the women's time of Mary Meagher (U.S.A.) is 57.93 sec. Freestyle records for 100 meters are 48.52 sec held by America's Dave McCagg and 54.04 sec by East German's Birgit Neike. So one can see how much the Fly has progressed in a comparatively short time.

Since 1956, when butterfly was accepted as a separate event and stroke, its development has progressed rapidly. In its early days, the stroke was used with a breaststroke kick, by good breaststroke kickers, lacking ankle flexibility. However, with the increased use of the dolphin kick and the stroke's demand for great flexibility in arms and shoulders, more and more front crawl swimmers adapted to butterfly. Also, as individual medley swimming developed, so did the butterfly stroke.

The stroke calls for great flexibility, co-ordination and feel for the water. Attention must be paid in all the drills, to perform the movements in such a manner that will transfer to a good fluent stroke.

Fly Kicking Drills:

1. Using a kick-board, arms at full extension, with elbows behind end of board, kick dolphin, head up ("bounce the feet up").

2. Drill 1 with head down, raising it for a breath every second kick, and dropping it down sharply for exhalation. ("Use back in movement.")

3. Kick dolphin, with arms extended (no board) head up, to increase resistance and power in legs.

4. Kick dolphin, face in water, breathe every second kick, ("head down and feet down as bottoms up").

5. With arms at sides, face in water, kick dolphin, (accentuate use of back in movement).

6. As drill 5, insist on chin pushing forward on surface for breath.

7. As drill 6 insist on quick return of head into water after breath.

8. As drill 7, but breathe every 4th kick. (Kick must be continuous throughout.)

9. On back, arms at side, kick dolphin (improves sensation of dolphin like movement through the body).

10. Dolphin kick, under water, arms outstretched, hands together, to help the streamline position and to help get "long" dolphin feel.

11. Dolphin kick, under water, arms at side, kick fast, to experience speed of

movement.

12. With arms at sides, dolphin kick while lying on right side. (Keep back straight so that movement of whole leg may be felt.)

13. Repeat drill 12, but work on left side.

14. Kick 25 right side, 25 on back, 25 on left side and 25 on front.

15. Use fins in any of the kicking drills to assist flexibility of ankles.

Fly Arms Drills:

1. Using dolphin kick, left arm out in front, pull with right arm. Describe the arm recovery as Fly (i.e., elbow raised from water and hand swung round low, to enter thumb first). Breathe to side after pull, *making sure* the head is quickly returned to water before hand entry.

2. Drill 1 using left arm to pull.

3. Using pull buoy, repeat drill 1.

4. Using pull buoy, repeat drill 2.

5. Using pull buoy and rubber band repeat drill 1.

6. Using pull buoy and rubber band repeat drill 2. Exercises 3 to 6 are for strengthening arms.

7. Using pull buoy, swim three right arm, three left arm Fly. (Remember to get head back before hand entry.)

8. Using pull buoy, any combination or series of combinations of single arm pulling.

9. Using pull buoys, swim three right arm, three left arm, three full stroke and continue for length of pool. (Head back before hands enter. Talk about digging a hole in the chest with chin.)

10. Using pull buoy, swim full stroke Fly, breathing every stroke, by stretching neck to place chin on surface.

11. As drill 10 breathe every second stroke.

12. Employ exercises 7 to 11 using dolphin kick.

13. Swim butterfly dolphin, allowing swimmers to breathe at will (establish own patterns).

14. On back, dolphin kick with double arm Backstroke. (Helps flexibility of shoulders and timing of kick.)

15. Swim front crawl arms with dolphin kick. (Improves co-ordination and develops kick at speed.)

16. Swim lengths of pool counting pulls and reduce until the minimum number is arrived at while remained proficient.

Timing and coordination for Fly:

1. One arm Fly swim, other hand at side, no breathing.

2. One arm Fly swim, other hand at side, breathe to side, after pull with head returned before hand.

3. One arm Fly swim, breathe to front, chin on water, neck stretched.

4. Swim full stroke, breathe only when absolutely necessary (chin on water).

5. Swim full stroke, breathe every third stroke.

6. Swim full stroke, breathe at will.

7. Swim drill 6 using fists (brings in use of forearms and helps arm bend in initial part of pull).

8. Swim drill 6 with clenched fists until the hands reach the hip line, from where the stroke is continued with open hands.

A well-used quote in butterfly instruction, which I believe is the key to good stroke is to "raise the head before the hands leave the water, and get it in before the hands enter the water."

9. Dive butterfly is a drill which helps the development of the technique and the ability to swim distance on butterfly. With the arms extended in front, the swimmer pushes off under water, does three or four dolphin kicks, surfaces and then with a butterfly recovery of the arms dives down again for a further three or four kicks and so on for 100 or 200 meters. Remember to come up to pull.

10. As above exercise but reduce the number of kicks.

11. Continue drills 9 and 10 over a period until the normal two beat kick stroke arrives with the shallow dive.

12. Eventually from this, a 200 meter Fly swimmer can be developed.

13. A combination of good quantity for the exercises would be 25 meters right arm Fly, 50 meters dive Fly, 25 meters left arm Fly, 25 meters full stroke, 50 meters dive Fly, 25 meters full stroke.

Starts and Turns for Fly:

1. For the starts, use cross pool swimming, getting out by placing hands on deck and raising body out of the water (as butterfly pull). Use two undulating kicks after speed of glide from entry has diminished then one stroke before breath. In the case of poor kickers, encourage flatter entry and starting with a strong arm movement.

Turning in Butterfly does not seem to get as much attention as say the front crawl tumble turn, yet so much depends on a good Fly turn to help keep the momentum of the stroke going.

2. From five or more meters out from wall swim in Fly, practicing to reach the trough or wall at comfortable entry position. If half a stroke must be made it should be made earlier, so that the stroke prior to turning is "on". This practice should be done regularly until a habit is formed.

3. Practice turns from five yards out dropping on right stroke, turning, push off with two undulating kicks, then pull and breathe.

Breaststroke

Of all the four strokes, the rule book most precisely describes breaststroke. It also seems to have been changing regularly over the years. Today, there are two distinct methods in use in World Competition the "natural" method, as used by David Wilkie and Tracy Caulkins and many of the Russian and East Germans, noticeable, for its high bobbing action, and the formal method, which as its name implies, is nearer to the flat body position breaststroke used for years, and favored by the U.S.A. However, there are successful swimmers in all parts of the world using one or the other of these methods.

For the youngster in training, the drills and techniques needed to develop a good stroke are not necessarily altered. Leg kicks have to be made legal and strong, arms and upper body strengthened, timing perfected and the breathing injected before either method is ready for adoption.

Breaststroke Kicking Drills:

1. Using kick board, arms at full stretch, kick breaststroke, head up, chin out of water.

2. Kick breaststroke, using board with face in the water (accentuate glide to develop streamlining of body).

3. Kick breaststroke, using board, face in water breathe every second kick.

4. Kick breaststroke, with board, breathing every kick (chin on water to breathe, face on water to breathe out).

5. Using board, kick breaststroke counting kicks.

6. As drill 5, try to kick one less (develop strength in leg drive) proceed until swimmer has got the minimum number of kicks, and remains proficient.

7. Holding kick board at right angles to water surface, kick breaststroke (develops power of kick).

8. Arms extended, face on water, kick breaststroke, raising chin out of water to breathe.

9. Arms extended, chin on water, kick breaststroke (develops power of kick).

10. With arms at sides, fingers pointing to feet, kick breaststroke. touching feet to fingers before kicking (regularizes kick, keeps knees narrower, and strengthens kick). Face in water raising chin to breathe.

11. As drill 10, but keep chin on water. (Power increase.)

12. Swimmer on back, hands and arms extended on water, kick breaststroke (keep knees below surface, and whip the kick below knees).

Head should be raised forward in this above drill.

13. As exercise 12, with arms half-way extended, and kick breaststroke, (increases resistance to kick).

14. On right side, with hands and arms close to sides pointing to feet, kick breaststroke, having feet touch fingers before kick.

15. As drill 14 on left side.

16. A combination of drills 10 to 15 would give the basis of a kicking drill series vis a vis: 25 on right side, hands and arms at sides feet touch to hands, 25 on back, 25 on left side and 25 on front.

17. Breaststroke kick using three different board combinations, as; two boards fastened together or three boards fastened.

Helps to keep shoulders out out water, keeps an open angle between hips and torso and develops a higher catch of the feet before each kick.

18. Using one kick board, one-legged breaststroke kick.

19. Using kick board, kick each leg alternately, "egg beater" kick.

20. Arms extended, "egg beater" kick.

21. Upright, in deep water, with hands upon head, kick breaststroke, keeping waist above surface.

22. As in 21 but using "egg beater" kick. (Helps to develop "feel" for feet.)

23. Using exercise 21 travel across deep end of pool.

24. Using exercise 22 go across deep end of pool.

Breaststroke Arms Drills:

1. Laying over a lane rope practice breaststroke arm pull. (Keep elbows in front of shoulders in recovery.)

2. Using pull buoy, pull breaststroke, head up.

3. Using pull buoy, pull breaststroke, face in water, breathing every stroke.

4. As in previous drill, but breathe every second pull. (Look for late breath.)

5. Discard pull buoy, trail legs and pull breaststroke. (Increases resistance.)

6. Discard pull buoy, pull breaststroke with legs apart in V shape. (Further increases resistance.)

7. Repeat drill 5 and 6 but breathe every second stroke.

8. With rubber band around knees, pull breaststroke, head up.

9. As in drill 8 but with head down, breathing every stroke.

10. Discard bands, pull breaststroke fast, introducing a small dolphin-like kick (speeds up movement), head up.

11. As in practice 10 but with face in water, breathing every stroke.

12. Using pull buoy again, leave left arm outstretched and use right arm only (isolates the movement).

13. Using pull buoy, land now pull left arm.

14. Combining 12 and 13 pull three right, three left, or whatever combination required. (Isolates arms and adds variety.)

15. For a series component, 25 yards, pull three right, three left, 25 yards, pulling both, 25 yards, right arm only, 25 yards, left arm only.

16. Pull breaststroke, legs trailing (resistance).

17. Pull breaststroke, using pull buoy (resistance).

18. Pull breaststroke, using pull buoy and rubber band (resistance).

19. All the three exercises 16,17,18 using fists.

20. Partner holding ankles, pull breaststroke (resistance).

21. Tie a short rope (about 18") to a couple of tubes, which two swimmers will don - one each - then from center of pool have them pull against each other. If either pulls the other to end of pool, then return to middle again and recommence. Practice heads in water, breathing every two.

22. Practice as above but with heads out of water.

Timing and coordination for Breaststroke:

It was once thought that to be a class breaststroker, a swimmer needed a very powerful leg kick, and indeed, in the pre-Jastremski period, little importance was put on arms-only drills in breaststroke. As a consequence, I believe, most breaststrokers kicked hard, glided and took an early breath in the arm pull. However, with the advent of the Jastremski influence where the premise was that the arms should contribute substantially to propulsion, the breaststroke of the kicker was revolutionized.

Since that time we have had further changes, and now we have two recognized schools of breaststroke, the "formal" method, and the "natural" method. But whatever school is favored, it is accepted by all the top coaches that the timing of the stroke is the key to being successful. Thus, it happens, that a swimmer may not be a strong breaststroke kicker or he may not be very powerful arms swimmer, but yet when he puts the stroke together, with the correct timing, he becomes championship material.

Timing and coordination drills for Breaststroke:

1. Kick breaststroke, arms outstretched, hand upon hand, slowly introduce a small arm stroke (as though caressing a tennis ball).

2. As in previous drill but increase arm stroke (caress a football).

3. Same as 1 and 2 start, but arrive at full arm stroke (caress a large beach

ball). Develops coordination and teaches feel of arm movement.

4. Swim breaststroke, breathing every third stroke. (Helps to establish late breathing.)

5. As drill 4 breathe every second stroke as when shoulders are highest.

6. Swim breaststroke, breathe every stroke as taken in drill 5 and 6.

7. Arms extended, hand over hand, kick three breaststrokes, pull one arm movement and breathe, then kick three breaststrokes and so on. (Helps place breathing and is also a great conditioner.)

8. As 7 but kick twice, pull twice, kick twice.

9. Swim breaststroke, kick two breaststrokes to one pull.

10. Swim breaststroke, with two pulls to one kick.

11. A combination of 9 and 10, two kicks one pull, one kick two pulls.

12. Swim breaststroke, crossing arms over prior to pull. (Helps straighten arms at beginning of pull, and assists the timing of the stroke.)

13. Swim breaststroke, take a long glide on each stroke to a count of 400, 300, 200, 100.

14. As drill 13 but count from 300 to 100. Numbers to be said in words.

15. As drill 14 but count 200, 100.

16. Swim breaststroke glide to call 100.

17. Swim breaststroke, no glide, but retain extension of arms.

18. Swim one arm breaststroke, right arm extended, left arm working.

19. Swim one arm breaststroke, using opposite members.

20. One arm breaststroke. left arm at side, hand outstretched towards feet, swim with right arm, and bring left foot to touch left hand while progressing.

21. Opposite arms using practice 20.

22. Swim breaststroke using alternating single leg kicks, fitting in with normal stroke.

23. Swim breaststroke for four strokes under water, return to surface on wide arm pull, submerge again for four more strokes and so on (hypoxic work - breath control).

Breaststroke Turns:

1. From five yards out, swim breaststroke into wall, turn and push off and glide to a stop.

2. As drill 1 check when speed drops off then use underwater pull.

3. As drill 2 then add kick as arms stretch to full extension at the surface.

4. Check distance each time and try to improve.

5. Swim into wall from five yards out, turn, push off surface and sprint to other end.

6. Swim a series of such distances going at a set time. (Keep a watch on distance achieved from push.)

7. Swim widths of pool trying to maintain the same number of strokes throughout.

8. Underwater breaststroke across the pool, coming up for turns.

9. Time should be spent on practicing push-offs, especially for breaststrokers introducing underwater pull and kick to get the greatest distance possible.

Individual Medley (I.M.)

There is a place within medley training for the use of drills, combining some of those described in the strokes. These can be used for kicking or pulling, part stroke or full stroke.

1. Kick four by one I.M. as using arms outstretched, throughout. Develop to four by four.

2. Kick medley order on right side.

3. Kick medley order on left side.

4. Pull medley order using right arm only using pull.

5. Drill 4 left arm only.

6. Combination of arm movements as 3 right arm, 3 left arm.

7. Performs 4, 5 and 6 with kicking (discard pull buoys).

8. Swim single arm Fly, double arm back, breathe every two on Breast, and single arm front crawl. Combinations using different drills for each stroke may be used for the medley distance preferred.

9. A hypoxic practice for medley is to swim Fly breathing three, swim back holding breath for four strokes, under water Breast for four strokes and dive, breathe every five for front crawl.

In conclusion, this collection of drills is meant to be an aid to beginning coaches especially, and I hope they will serve that purpose. There is nothing new or original within this list. After more than thirty years in the business of developing strokes and swimmers at all levels, I am still seeking further new ways. Those I have listed, have come from years of teaching ten or eleven classes per day plus three hours coaching per evening, plus reading every swimming publication, attending clinics and talking swimming non-stop to the point of boring friends to tears. Often when one has thought that one has developed a new exciting drill, one would pick up a swimming book and find that very drill.

Most of my information for this collection has been derived from such notable people as Forbes Carlile, Don Gambril, Howard Firby, Cecil Colwin, Deryk Snelling and Dick Hannula, and from my many friends in the business of coaching swimming.

Chapter Seven
Workouts

Glossary of terms used in workout directions: The four strokes are referred to as Butterfly, Backstroke, Breaststroke, and Freestyle (accepted as front crawl). In contracted form they are:

FLY = Butterfly
BK = Backstroke
BR = Breaststroke
F/S = Freestyle (front crawl)

Individual Medley: - four equal distances using Butterfly, Backstroke, Breaststroke, and Freestyle to complete overall distances. The 400 I.M. is 100 yards of each stroke in the order as stated. (4 x 50) I.M. or 200 I.M. is 50 yards of each of the four strokes in order.

Stroke - where this word is used in the workouts, it infers other than Freestyle and usually the swimmer's best stroke.

Kick - evidently, means to use the legs, either using a kickboard for the arms, or locking the thumbs. No arm propulsion at all.

Pull - oppositely, denotes using the arms only. Often with legs tied and using a pull buoy.

Drill - is to detach a component of the stroke for special attention. For instance, a Backstroke drill is to swim Backstroke leaving one arm at the side, and using only the other. Kick as you would normally kick on the Backstroke. Similarly, the other strokes can be approached in the same manner.

To *reduce* - reference to a set of swims meaning to swim each successive distance faster. (Also referred to as *descend*.)

To *pace* - holding a segment of the racing distance at a steady rate, which the swimmer needs to attain a final goal time.

Breathe 3 (or 4 or 5 or 6) - when the swimmer takes his breath after that many strokes.

Parenthesis - around an instruction, [i.e., 8 X (50 BR + 50 F/S)] means that the swimmer must swim 50 BR followed by 50 F/S eight times, or simply that the work inside the bracket must be completed eight times.

Where there are *several sets of work within a bracket* as:

4 X (4 X 50 BK ON :45
(4 X 75 BR ON 1:20
(4 X 100 F/S ON 1:15)

means that the three sets of instructions must be completed in sequence and then repeated four times. Mathematics would have it as - remove all inside the brackets before multiplying.

To *build* - is to increase the pace of the swim from moderate to fast.

EZ - a phonetic explanation for easy.

Sprint - is just that - GO FOR IT!

I hope that whoever you are, you find this book, *Mastering Masters Swimming*, of some value. Most importantly, I hope that it helps you to get more enjoyment from your Master's program.

1. Mastering

SWIM:	500 YDS EZ USING ALL 4 STROKES
SWIM:	400 YDS IM, REST 5 SECS AFTER EACH 25 FLY
KICK:	(50 FLY + 50 BK + 50 BR) ON 3:00
KICK:	(50 BK + 50 BR + 50 F/S) ON 3:00
PULL:	4 X (200 F/S + 50 STROKE) ON 3:45
SWIM:	6 X (25 FLY + 100 BK + 25 BR) ON 2:45
DRILL:	100 IM
SWIM:	8 X 50 F/S ON :50 - HOLDING :37
SWIM:	EZ 200 YDS CHOICE

1. Mastering

SWIM:	500 YDS EZ USING ALL 4 STROKES
SWIM:	400 YDS IM, REST 5 SECS AFTER EACH 25 FLY
KICK:	(50 FLY + 50 BK + 50 BR) ON 3:00
KICK:	(50 BK + 50 BR + 50 F/S) ON 3:00
PULL:	4 X (200 F/S + 50 STROKE) ON 3:45
SWIM:	6 X (25 FLY + 100 BK + 25 BR) ON 2:45
DRILL:	100 IM
SWIM:	8 X 50 F/S ON :50 - HOLDING :37
SWIM:	EZ 200 YDS CHOICE

As ye swim in practice, so shall ye swim in meets.

86. Mastering

SWIM:	1,000 YDS EZ 3 STROKES WARM UP
K/P	5 X (KICK 100, PULL 100) ON 4:00 USE ALL STROKES
SWIM:	6 X 200 ODD# F/S ON 3:00 EVEN # BK OR BR ON 3:30
PULL:	(100 F/S + 100 IM) X 3 ON 3:15
SPRINT:	4 X 50 STROKE ON 1:15 DESCEND TIME
SWIM:	DOWN EZ 200 F/S

2. Mastering

SWIM: 500 YDS EZ WARM-UP ALL STROKES
(KICK 100, PULL 100) IM ORDER
WITH 10 SEC REST BETWEEN EACH STROKE AND 5 SEC AT EACH 25

SWIM: 4 X 100 IM ON 2:00

PULL: (100 BR + 200 F/S)X 4
WITH 10 SEC REST AFTER EACH 300

SWIM: 10 X 50 F/S ON :55 (500 PACE OF :39)

KICK: 100 FLY + 100 BK + 200 BR + 100 F/S

SWIM: DOWN EZ 200 CHOICE

2. Mastering

SWIM: 500 YDS EZ WARM-UP ALL STROKES
(KICK 100, PULL 100) IM ORDER
WITH 10 SEC REST BETWEEN EACH STROKE AND 5 SEC AT EACH 25

SWIM: 4 X 100 IM ON 2:00

PULL: (100 BR + 200 F/S)X 4
WITH 10 SEC REST AFTER EACH 300

SWIM: 10 X 50 F/S ON :55 (500 PACE OF :39)

KICK: 100 FLY + 100 BK + 200 BR + 100 F/S

SWIM: DOWN EZ 200 CHOICE

Biting off more than you can chew is better than going hungry.

87. Mastering

SWIM:	500 YDS F/S EZ WARM UP
KICK:	8 X 50 CHOICE ON 1:00
PULL:	6 X 100 F/S ON 1:45
DRILL:	4 X 100 IM ORDER ON 2:00
SWIM:	6 X (100 IM ON 1:45 + 100 F/S ON 1:30)
SWIM:	12 X 50 ON 1:15 USE 2 STROKES, NO F/S
SWIM:	DOWN EZ 200 F/S

3. Mastering

SWIM: 500 YDS EZ ALL STROKES
KICK: (50 FLY + 50 BK),
(50 BK + 50 BR),
(50 BR + 50 F/S)
WITH 10 SEC REST AT EACH 100 - REPEAT
SWIM: 16 X 25 ON :30, ALTERNATE F/S AND STROKE
PULL: 500 F/S ON 7:00, BREATHE 3 & 5 PER 100
SWIM: 2 X (100 FLY + 200 BK + 100 F/S) ON 7:00
SWIM: 2 X 200 BR ON 3:45
KICK: 16 X 25 ON :40, ALTERNATE F/S AND CHOICE
SWIM: 10 X 50 F/S ON :50, HOLD :37
SWIM: DOWN EZ 200 CHOICE

3. Mastering

SWIM: 500 YDS EZ ALL STROKES
KICK: (50 FLY + 50 BK),
(50 BK + 50 BR),
(50 BR + 50 F/S)
WITH 10 SEC REST AT EACH 100 - REPEAT
SWIM: 16 X 25 ON :30, ALTERNATE F/S AND STROKE
PULL: 500 F/S ON 7:00, BREATHE 3 & 5 PER 100
SWIM: 2 X (100 FLY + 200 BK + 100 F/S) ON 7:00
SWIM: 2 X 200 BR ON 3:45
KICK: 16 X 25 ON :40, ALTERNATE F/S AND CHOICE
SWIM: 10 X 50 F/S ON :50, HOLD :37
SWIM: DOWN EZ 200 CHOICE

Be realistic —— demand the impossible.

88. Mastering

SWIM:	500 YDS F/S AND #1 STROKE EZ
KICK:	5 X 100 ALTERNATE FLY & F/S ON 2:00
PULL:	8 X (25 BR + 150 F/S) ON 2:45
SWIM:	6 X 100 BK ON 2:00
SWIM:	6 X 100 BR ON 2:00
SWIM:	8 X 75 F/S 4 ON 1:00, 4 ON 1:05
DRILL:	200 IM
SWIM:	4 X (25 F/S ON :30 + 25 FLY ON :30)
SWIM:	DOWN EZ 200 CHOICE

4. Mastering

SWIM:	500 YDS EZ WARM-UP USE ALL 4 STROKES
KICK:	8 X 100 ON 2:00, ALTERNATE IM AND CHOICE
DRILL:	100 BK
SWIM:	20 X 25 ON :30, IM ORDER
PULL:	4 X 200 F/S, *BREATHE 4 & 6 PER 100 WITH 10 SEC REST AT 200*
SWIM:	2 X (100 FLY + 200 BR + 100 F/S) ON 7:00
SWIM:	8 x 50 BK ON 1:00
SWIM:	10 X 50 F/S, 6 ON :50, 4 ON :45
SWIM:	DOWN EZ 200 CHOICE

4. Mastering

SWIM:	500 YDS EZ WARM-UP USE ALL 4 STROKES
KICK:	8 X 100 ON 2:00, ALTERNATE IM AND CHOICE
DRILL:	100 BK
SWIM:	20 X 25 ON :30, IM ORDER
PULL:	4 X 200 F/S, *BREATHE 4 & 6 PER 100 WITH 10 SEC REST AT 200*
SWIM:	2 X (100 FLY + 200 BR + 100 F/S) ON 7:00
SWIM:	8 x 50 BK ON 1:00
SWIM:	10 X 50 F/S, 6 ON :50, 4 ON :45
SWIM:	DOWN EZ 200 CHOICE

Be consistently persistent.
Dick Hannula

89. Mastering

SWIM:	500 YDS CHOICE EZ
SWIM:	8 X 50 F/S ON :50
KICK:	4 X 50 FLY
	4 X 50 FLY OR BK
	4 X 50 BK
	4 X 50 BR
	4 X 50 F/S
	ALL ABOVE ON 1:00
PULL:	10 X (25 STROKE + 25 BR + 50 F/S) ON 1:55
SWIM:	10 X (25 BK + 25 BR + 50 F/S) ON 1:40
SWIM:	4 X 50 FLY ON 1:30 DESCEND
SWIM:	DOWN EZ 200 STROKE

5. Mastering

SWIM:	500 YDS EZ WARM UP USE ALL STROKES
PULL:	3 X 300 F/S USING PULL BUOY ON 4:30
	BREATHE 4 & 6 PER 150
SWIM:	8 X 25 FLY ON :35
KICK:	4 X 200 IM ORDER ON 4:15
SWIM:	200 FLY + 100 BK + 100 BR ON 7:15
	100 FLY + 200 BK + 100 BR ON 7:15
	200 BK + 100 BR + 100 F/S ON 7:00
	100 BK + 200 BR + 100 F/S ON 7:00
SPRINT:	4 X 50 STROKE ON 1:00
SWIM:	DOWN EZ 200 CHOICE

5. Mastering

SWIM:	500 YDS EZ WARM UP USE ALL STROKES
PULL:	3 X 300 F/S USING PULL BUOY ON 4:30
	BREATHE 4 & 6 PER 150
SWIM:	8 X 25 FLY ON :35
KICK:	4 X 200 IM ORDER ON 4:15
SWIM:	200 FLY + 100 BK + 100 BR ON 7:15
	100 FLY + 200 BK + 100 BR ON 7:15
	200 BK + 100 BR + 100 F/S ON 7:00
	100 BK + 200 BR + 100 F/S ON 7:00
SPRINT:	4 X 50 STROKE ON 1:00
SWIM:	DOWN EZ 200 CHOICE

A team which has become a winner has done so by certain individuals setting and reaching goals for themselves.

90. Mastering

SWIM:	500 YDS EZ WARM UP
KICK:	10 X 50 F/S ON 1:00
SWIM:	20 X 50 F/S
	ON :50 AND :45 ALTERNATELY
PULL:	6 X (100 STROKE + 100 F/S) ON 3:30
SWIM:	IM:200 BK *TECHNIQUE* SWIM
	ON 3:45
SWIM:	200 BR TECHNIQUE SWIM ON 3:45
SPRINT:	16 X 25 IM ORDER ON :40
SWIM:	DOWN EZ 200 STROKE

6. Mastering

SWIM:	500 YDS EZ WARM-UP
KICK:	8 X 100 CHOICE ON 2:00
PULL:	8 X 100 F/S ON 1:45, *BREATHE 2,3,4,5 AND 7 PER 100*
SWIM:	4 X (100 FLY + 100 BK) ON 4:15
	4 X (100 BK + 100 BR) ON 4:00
	4 X (100 BR + 100 F/S) ON 3:45
SWIM:	DOWN EZ 200 F/S

6. Mastering
SWIM: 500 YDS EZ WARM-UP
KICK: 8 X 100 CHOICE ON 2:00
PULL: 8 X 100 F/S ON 1:45, *BREATHE 2,3,4,5 AND 7 PER 100*
SWIM: 4 X (100 FLY + 100 BK) ON 4:15
4 X (100 BK + 100 BR) ON 4:00
4 X (100 BR + 100 F/S) ON 3:45
SWIM: DOWN EZ 200 F/S

Anyone who thinks the sky is the limit has limited imagination.

91. Mastering

SWIM:	500 YDS CHOICE EZ WARM UP
SWIM:	4 X 150 F/S ON 2:10
DRILL:	100 BK
KICK:	12 X 50 ALTERNATE F/S AND BEST STROKE ON 1:00
PULL:	4 X 200 F/S ON 3:00 *BREATHE 5,7 PER 100*
SWIM:	8 X (150 F/S ON 2:05 + 50 STROKE ON 1:00)
SPRINT:	4 X 25 F/S ON :30 HOLD :17
SWIM:	DOWN EZ 200 F/S

7.Mastering

SWIM:	500 YDS EZ CHOICE
SWIM:	2 X 150 F/S ON 2:05
	2 X 75 ON 1:05
	2 X 25 ON :25
	NO REST BETWEEN SETS = 500
KICK:	400 IM ON 8:30
DRILL:	100 CHOICE
SWIM:	2 X 150 ON 2:00
	2 X 75 ON 1:00
	2 X 25 ON :25
	NO REST BETWEEN SETS = 500
SWIM:	100 STROKE EZ
PULL:	2 X (200 F/S + 50 STROKE) ON 3:45
SWIM:	8 X (25 FLY + 25 BK + 25 BR) ON 1:30
	8 X (25 BK + 25 BR + 25 F/S) ON 1:20
SWIM:	DOWN EZ 200 F/S

7.Mastering

SWIM:	500 YDS EZ CHOICE
SWIM:	2 X 150 F/S ON 2:05
	2 X 75 ON 1:05
	2 X 25 ON :25
	NO REST BETWEEN SETS = 500
KICK:	400 IM ON 8:30
DRILL:	100 CHOICE
SWIM:	2 X 150 ON 2:00
	2 X 75 ON 1:00
	2 X 25 ON :25
	NO REST BETWEEN SETS = 500
SWIM:	100 STROKE EZ
PULL:	2 X (200 F/S + 50 STROKE) ON 3:45
SWIM:	8 X (25 FLY + 25 BK + 25 BR) ON 1:30
	8 X (25 BK + 25 BR + 25 F/S) ON 1:20
SWIM:	DOWN EZ 200 F/S

Oh, boy, is this great!
Flounder, Animal House

92. Mastering

SWIM:	500 YDS EZ WARM UP
SWIM:	4 X (75 F/S ON 1:00 + 25 F/S EZ ON :30)
KICK:	8 X 75 CHOICE ON 1:25
PULL:	4 X (100 F/S + 100 IM) ON 3:15
SWIM:	8 X 50 FLY OR WORST STROKE 4 ON 1:00, 4 ON 1:15
SWIM:	5 X 300 F/S ON 4:20
SWIM:	DOWN EZ 200 STROKE

8. Mastering

SWIM:	500 YDS EZ F/S
KICK:	5 X 100 ALTERNATE IM AND CHOICE ON 2:05
PULL:	3 X 200 F/S ON 3:00, *BREATHE 3 & 5 PER 100*
SWIM:	200 IM + 50 FLY ON 4:30
	200 IM + 50 BK ON 4:30
	200 IM + 50 BR ON 4:30
	200 IM + 50 F/S ON 4:15
DRILL:	200 BK
SWIM:	4 X (200 STROKE ON 3:45 + 50 F/S ON :45)
KICK:	200 F/S AS 25 EZ, 25 FAST
SPRINT:	4 X 25 F/S ON :30 DESCEND TO :16
SWIM:	DOWN EZ 200 STROKE

8. Mastering

SWIM:	500 YDS EZ F/S
KICK:	5 X 100 ALTERNATE IM AND CHOICE ON 2:05
PULL:	3 X 200 F/S ON 3:00, *BREATHE 3 & 5 PER 100*
SWIM:	200 IM + 50 FLY ON 4:30
	200 IM + 50 BK ON 4:30
	200 IM + 50 BR ON 4:30
	200 IM + 50 F/S ON 4:15
DRILL:	200 BK
SWIM:	4 X (200 STROKE ON 3:45 + 50 F/S ON :45)
KICK:	200 F/S AS 25 EZ, 25 FAST
SPRINT:	4 X 25 F/S ON :30 DESCEND TO :16
SWIM:	DOWN EZ 200 STROKE

Winning tastes good.
Jean-Claude Killy

93. Mastering

SWIM:	500 YDS USE ALL 4 STROKES
SWIM:	8 X 50 F/S ON :45
DRILL:	200 IM KICK:
	6 X 100 FLY & BK ALTERNATELY ON 2:00
SWIM:	4 X (50 FLY + 150 BK) ON 3:45
PULL:	8 X 75 F/S ON 1:05 *BREATHE 5*
SWIM:	6 X (50 BR + 75 F/S) ON 2:00
SPRINT:	4 X 75 F/S ON 1:15 HOLD :57
SWIM:	DOWN EZ 200 F/S

9. Mastering

SWIM: 500 YDS EZ WARM-UP
SWIM: 10 X 50 F/S ON :50
KICK: 2 X (50 FLY + 100 BK + 50 BR + 100 F/S) ON 6:00
DRILL: 100 BK
PULL: 2 X (350 F/S + 50 BR) ON 6:30
BREATHE:EVERY 3RD ON F/S AND EVERY 2ND ON BR
SWIM: 10 X 100, ALTERNATE IM ON 1:45, AND F/S ON 1:30
SWIM: 200 STROKE EZ
SWIM: 8 X 25 FLY ON :40
4 X 50 BK ON 1:00
4 X 50 BR ON 1:00
SWIM: DOWN EZ 200 F/S

9. Mastering

SWIM: 500 YDS EZ WARM-UP
SWIM: 10 X 50 F/S ON :50
KICK: 2 X (50 FLY + 100 BK + 50 BR + 100 F/S) ON 6:00
DRILL: 100 BK
PULL: 2 X (350 F/S + 50 BR) ON 6:30
BREATHE:EVERY 3RD ON F/S AND EVERY 2ND ON BR
SWIM: 10 X 100, ALTERNATE IM ON 1:45, AND F/S ON 1:30
SWIM: 200 STROKE EZ
SWIM: 8 X 25 FLY ON :40
4 X 50 BK ON 1:00
4 X 50 BR ON 1:00
SWIM: DOWN EZ 200 F/S

You are what you are and you are where you are because of what has gone into your mind. You change what you are and you change where you are by changing what goes into your mind.
Zig Ziglar

94. Mastering

SWIM:	500 YDS EZ WARM UP
SWIM:	100 F/S ON 1:25
	2 X 75 F/S ON 1:00
	3 X 50 F/S ON :40
	4 X 25 F/S ON :25
KICK:	12 X 50 IM ORDER ON 1:05
PULL:	4 X 300 F/S ON 4:45
	BREATHE 3,4,5 PER 100
SWIM:	4 X (25 FLY ON :30 + 100 BK ON 1:50)
SPRINT:	4 X 50 STROKE ON 1:15 DESCEND
SWIM:	DOWN EZ 200 STROKE

10. Mastering

SWIM:	500 YDS EZ WARM-UP
PULL:	8 X 100 F/S ON 1:30
SWIM:	12 X 25 STROKE (HARD) ON :30
KICK:	3 X (100 STROKE + 100 F/S) ON 4:15
SWIM:	4 X 100 IM ON 1:45
	2 X 200 IM ON 3:45
	1 X 400 IM ON 7:00
DRILL:	200 IM REVERSE ORDER
SPRINT:	16 X 25 ON :30,
	ALTERNATE CHOICE AND F/S
SWIM:	DOWN EZ 200 CHOICE

10. Mastering

SWIM:	500 YDS EZ WARM-UP
PULL:	8 X 100 F/S ON 1:30
SWIM:	12 X 25 STROKE (HARD) ON :30
KICK:	3 X (100 STROKE + 100 F/S) ON 4:15
SWIM:	4 X 100 IM ON 1:45
	2 X 200 IM ON 3:45
	1 X 400 IM ON 7:00
DRILL:	200 IM REVERSE ORDER
SPRINT:	16 X 25 ON :30,
	ALTERNATE CHOICE AND F/S
SWIM:	DOWN EZ 200 CHOICE

Don't try to duplicate past performances; just do the best you can today.

95. Mastering

SWIM:	500 YDS USE STROKES & DRILLS
SWIM:	6 X (125 F/S ON 1:40 +
	75 F/S ON 1:05 +
	50 F/S ON :40 +
	25 F/S ON :30)
	NO REST IN BETWEEN SETS
DRILL:	6 X 50 BK ON 1:00
SWIM:	6 X (125 F/S ON 1:45 +
	75 F/S ON 1:10 +
	50 F/S ON:45 +
	25 F/S ON :30)
	NO REST IN BETWEEN SETS
SWIM:	DOWN EZ 200 F/S

11. Mastering

SWIM: 500 YDS EZ WARM-UP
4 X (KICK 100, PULL 100) IM ORDER
ON 4:00

SWIM: 10 X (25 BR + 100 F/S) ON 2:00
10 X (25 BK + 50 F/S) ON 1:30
10 X (25 BR + 25 F/S) ON 1:00

SPRINT: 6 X 25, ALTERNATE FLY AND BK
ON :40

SWIM: DOWN EZ 200

11. Mastering

SWIM: 500 YDS EZ WARM-UP
4 X (KICK 100, PULL 100) IM ORDER
ON 4:00

SWIM: 10 X (25 BR + 100 F/S) ON 2:00
10 X (25 BK + 50 F/S) ON 1:30
10 X (25 BR + 25 F/S) ON 1:00

SPRINT: 6 X 25, ALTERNATE FLY AND BK
ON :40

SWIM: DOWN EZ 200

It takes patience to endure the monotony of repetition.

96. Mastering

SWIM:	500 YDS F/S WITH DRILLS WARM UP
KICK:	10 X 50 F/S
	ON :55 AND 1:05 ALTERNATELY
DRILL:	4 X 25 IM ORDER ON :30
SWIM:	12 X 50 IM ORDER ON 1:00
PULL:	6 X (25 FLY + 100 F/S + 25 BR) ON 3:15
SWIM:	8 X 75 F/S 6 ON 1:00, 2 ON 1:05
SWIM:	4 X 50 BK ON 1:00 DESCEND
SWIM:	4 X 50 BR ON 1:00 DESCEND
SWIM:	8 X 25 F/S ON :30 HOLD :17
SWIM:	DOWN EZ 200 STROKE

12. Mastering

SWIM: 500 YDS WARM-UP
SWIM: 4 X 75 STROKE ON 1:30
KICK: 8 X 75, ALTERNATE F/S AND CHOICE ON 1:45
DRILL: 200 IM
PULL: 5 X (50 BR + 50 F/S) ON 2:00
BREATHE EVERY 5TH STROKE F/S
SWIM: 25 YDS + 5 SEC +
50 YDS + 5 SEC +
75 YDS + 5 SEC UP TO 275 YDS -
THIS IS 1 LAP, 2 LAP,3 LAP, 11 LAPS AS IF SWIMMING 1650. DEDUCT :50 TO GIVE TIME
SPRINT: 6 X 50 ALTERNATE F/S AND STROKE ON 1:00
SWIM: DOWN EZ 200

12. Mastering

SWIM: 500 YDS WARM-UP
SWIM: 4 X 75 STROKE ON 1:30
KICK: 8 X 75, ALTERNATE F/S AND CHOICE ON 1:45
DRILL: 200 IM
PULL: 5 X (50 BR + 50 F/S) ON 2:00
BREATHE EVERY 5TH STROKE F/S
SWIM: 25 YDS + 5 SEC +
50 YDS + 5 SEC +
75 YDS + 5 SEC UP TO 275 YDS -
THIS IS 1 LAP, 2 LAP,3 LAP, 11 LAPS AS IF SWIMMING 1650. DEDUCT :50 TO GIVE TIME
SPRINT: 6 X 50 ALTERNATE F/S AND STROKE ON 1:00
SWIM: DOWN EZ 200

Progress is our most important product.

97. Mastering

SWIM:	500 YDS USE 2 STROKES
SWIM:	8 X 50 F/S ON :45 HOLD :38
PULL:	6 X 150 F/S ON 2:10
	BREATHE 3,4,5 PER 100
KICK:	10 X 100
	ALTERNATE CHOICE AND F/S
	ON 2:00
SWIM:	4 X 125 BEST STROKE NO F/S
	ON 3:00 95 % EFFORT! !
SWIM:	4 X 50 WORST STROKE
	FOR TECHNIQUE
	WITH 10 SEC REST
SPRINT:	(30 F/S FAST + 20 F/S EZ) X 4 ON 1:15
	FAST IN AND OUT OF FLIP TURNS
SWIM:	DOWN EZ 200 F/S

13. Mastering

SWIM: 500 YDS EZ
SWIM: 8 X 50 F/S ON :45
KICK: 8 X 100 IM ON 2:00
PULL: 2 X (300 F/S + 100 BR) ON 7:00
SWIM: 8 X (25 FLY + 50 BK + 75 BR + 100 F/S) ON 4:30
SWIM: 3 X 200 F/S ON 3:30 DESCEND TIME
SWIM: DOWN EZ 200

13. Mastering

SWIM: 500 YDS EZ
SWIM: 8 X 50 F/S ON :45
KICK: 8 X 100 IM ON 2:00
PULL: 2 X (300 F/S + 100 BR) ON 7:00
SWIM: 8 X (25 FLY + 50 BK + 75 BR + 100 F/S) ON 4:30
SWIM: 3 X 200 F/S ON 3:30 DESCEND TIME
SWIM: DOWN EZ 200

Don't ever be caught doing nothing.

98. Mastering

SWIM:	500 YDS F/S AND DRILLS EZ
SWIM:	6 X 150 F/S ON 2:00
DRILL:	200 IM
SWIM:	3 X (25 F/S ON :20 + 100 IM ON 1:45 + 325 F/S ON 4:40 + 50 STROKE ON :50) *REST 30 SEC BETWEEN SETS*
KICK:	8 X (50 F/S + 25 CHOICE) ON 1:25
SPRINT:	4 X 75 STROKE ON 1:30 FAST
SWIM:	DOWN EZ 200 STROKE

14. Mastering

SWIM: 500 YDS EZ CHOICE
KICK: 2 X (3 X 100 ON 2:00 AS
50 FLY/50 BK,
50 BK/50 BR,
50 BR/50 F/S)
SWIM: 4 X (400 F/S ON 6:00 + 50 STROKE ON 1:00)
IN IM ORDER OR STROKE
PULL: 8 X 100 F/S ON 1:30,
BREATHE EVERY 5
SPRINT: 14 X 25 ON :30 - 2 FLY, 3 BK, 4 BR, 5 F/S
SWIM: DOWN EZ 200

14. Mastering

SWIM: 500 YDS EZ CHOICE
KICK: 2 X (3 X 100 ON 2:00 AS
50 FLY/50 BK,
50 BK/50 BR,
50 BR/50 F/S)
SWIM: 4 X (400 F/S ON 6:00 + 50 STROKE ON 1:00)
IN IM ORDER OR STROKE
PULL: 8 X 100 F/S ON 1:30,
BREATHE EVERY 5
SPRINT: 14 X 25 ON :30 - 2 FLY, 3 BK, 4 BR, 5 F/S
SWIM: DOWN EZ 200

It is better to have swum and lost than never to have swum at all.

99. Mastering

SWIM:	500 YDS ALL STROKES EZ
SWIM:	5 X 100 F/S ON 1:25 HOLD 1:16
KICK:	16 X 50 ON 1:00
	4 EACH STROKE IM ORDER
PULL:	5 X (100 STROKE + 100 F/S)
	ON 3:30
SWIM:	8 X (25 FLY + 50 BK) ON 1:20
SWIM:	5 X (25 BR + 75 F/S) ON 1:40
SPRINT:	4 X 25 STROKE ON :30
SWIM:	DOWN EZ 200 F/S

15. Mastering

SWIM: 500 YDS EZ F/S
DRILL: 400 IM
SWIM: 400 IM ON 7:00
KICK: 8 X 50 ON 1:10, ALTERNATE BK AND FLY-ON-BACK
PULL: 4 X 200 F/S ON 3:00, *BREATHE 4 & 6 PER 100*
KICK: 100 FLY + 200 BR + 100 F/S ON 8:00
SWIM: 4 X 300 AS (1)IM ON 5:30, (2)F/S ON 5:00 (3)IM ON 5:30 (4)F/S ON 5:00
SPRINT: 8 X 25 ON :45, ALTERNATE BK &BR
SWIM: DOWN EZ 200 F/S

15. Mastering

SWIM: 500 YDS EZ F/S
DRILL: 400 IM
SWIM: 400 IM ON 7:00
KICK: 8 X 50 ON 1:10, ALTERNATE BK AND FLY-ON-BACK
PULL: 4 X 200 F/S ON 3:00, *BREATHE 4 & 6 PER 100*
KICK: 100 FLY + 200 BR + 100 F/S ON 8:00
SWIM: 4 X 300 AS (1)IM ON 5:30, (2)F/S ON 5:00 (3)IM ON 5:30 (4)F/S ON 5:00
SPRINT: 8 X 25 ON :45, ALTERNATE BK &BR
SWIM: DOWN EZ 200 F/S

It is not how far you swim in practice, and it is not how fast you swim in practice. —— It's how far you swim fast.

100. Mastering

SWIM:	500 YDS F/S EZ
KICK:	8 X 75 CHOICE ON 1:30
SWIM:	6 X 50 ON :50 #1&2 FLY, 3 TO 6 F/S
DRILL:	200 BK
PULL:	200 BR + 300 F/S + 100 IM
KICK:	20 X 25 ON :30
	ROTATE CHOICE, BR, F/S, BR
SWIM:	8 X 125 F/S ON 2:00 HOLD 1:40
SWIM:	DOWN EZ 200 STROKE

16. Mastering

SWIM: 500 YDS EZ USE TWO DIFFERENT STROKES

SWIM: 1,000 F/S - BREAK AT 50 WITH
5 SEC REST
1,000 F/S - BREAK AT 100 WITH
5 SEC REST
1,000 F/S - BREAK AT 200 WITH
5 SEC REST
1,000 F/S - BREAK AT 250 WITH
5 SEC REST
1,000 F/S - BREAK AT 500 WITH
5 SEC REST
MAXIMUM REST BETWEEN SETS TO BE 15 SEC (1 HOUR SWIM PRACTICE)

SWIM: DOWN 200 NO F/S

16. Mastering

SWIM: 500 YDS EZ USE TWO DIFFERENT STROKES

SWIM: 1,000 F/S - BREAK AT 50 WITH
5 SEC REST
1,000 F/S - BREAK AT 100 WITH
5 SEC REST
1,000 F/S - BREAK AT 200 WITH
5 SEC REST
1,000 F/S - BREAK AT 250 WITH
5 SEC REST
1,000 F/S - BREAK AT 500 WITH
5 SEC REST
MAXIMUM REST BETWEEN SETS TO BE 15 SEC (1 HOUR SWIM PRACTICE)

SWIM: DOWN 200 NO F/S

Pretend you're a machine.

101. Mastering

SWIM:	500 YDS 4 STROKES AND DRILLS
SWIM:	100 F/S ON 1:30
	200 F/S ON 3:00
	300 F/S ON 4:30
	400 F/S ON 5:45
	500 F/S ON 7:00
	400 F/S ON 5:30
	300 F/S ON 4:15
	200 F/S ON 2:50
	100 F/S ON 1:25
DRILL:	200 IM
KICK:	400 IM
SWIM:	6 X 50 STROKE
	ON 1:00, DESCEND 1-3, 4-6
SWIM:	DOWN EZ 200 F/S

17. Mastering

SWIM:	500 YDS EZ WARM-UP ALL F/S
SWIM:	10 X 50 F/S - 3 ON :40, 3 ON :45, 4 ON :50
KICK:	6 X 100 ON 2:00, ALTERNATE F/S AND CHOICE
PULL:	4 X 200 F/S ON 2:55
SWIM:	12 X 100 ODD #S IM ON 1:45, EVEN #S STROKE ON 2:00
DRILL:	200 BK
SPRINT:	8 X 25 FLY ON :45
SWIM:	DOWN EZ 200

17. Mastering

SWIM:	500 YDS EZ WARM-UP ALL F/S
SWIM:	10 X 50 F/S - 3 ON :40, 3 ON :45, 4 ON :50
KICK:	6 X 100 ON 2:00, ALTERNATE F/S AND CHOICE
PULL:	4 X 200 F/S ON 2:55
SWIM:	12 X 100 ODD #S IM ON 1:45, EVEN #S STROKE ON 2:00
DRILL:	200 BK
SPRINT:	8 X 25 FLY ON :45
SWIM:	DOWN EZ 200

Aim at the stars. If you don't hit them, you'll land pretty high anyway.

102. Mastering

SWIM:	500 YDS EZ WARM UP
KICK:	75 FLY + 150 BK + 225 BR + 300 F/S ON 16:00
SWIM:	10 X 50 F/S ON :50 HOLD :36
DRILL:	4 X 50 BK ON 1:00
SWIM:	4 X (25 FLY ON :40 + 50 BK ON :50 + 50 BR ON :50 + 125 F/S ON 1:40)
PULL:	8 X 75 F/S ON 1:15 *BREATHE 3,4,5 PER 25*
SPRINT:	8 X (30 F/S + 20 BK EZ) ON 1:30 FAST IN & OUT OF FLIP TURNS
SWIM:	DOWN EZ 200 STROKE

18. Mastering

SWIM:	500 YDS EZ WARM-UP ALL STROKES
KICK:	5 X 100 ON 2:00 4 IN IM ORDER AND 1 100 IM
SWIM:	12 X 50 ON 1:00, 3 EACH STROKE IN IM ORDER
PULL:	4 X (150 F/S + 50 BR) ON 3:30, *BREATHE 3,5,7 PER 50 ON F/S AND EVERY 2ND STROKE BRST*
SWIM:	4 X 300 IM, SKIP STROKE ON EACH ON 5:15 (i.e OMIT FLY ON #1, BK ON #2, BR ON #3, AND F/S ON #4)
SWIM:	4 X 100 F/S ON 1:40 (HOLD 500 PACE)
SWIM:	DOWN EZ 200 STROKE

18. Mastering

SWIM:	500 YDS EZ WARM-UP ALL STROKES
KICK:	5 X 100 ON 2:00 4 IN IM ORDER AND 1 100 IM
SWIM:	12 X 50 ON 1:00, 3 EACH STROKE IN IM ORDER
PULL:	4 X (150 F/S + 50 BR) ON 3:30, *BREATHE 3,5,7 PER 50 ON F/S AND EVERY 2ND STROKE BRST*
SWIM:	4 X 300 IM, SKIP STROKE ON EACH ON 5:15 (i.e OMIT FLY ON #1, BK ON #2, BR ON #3, AND F/S ON #4)
SWIM:	4 X 100 F/S ON 1:40 (HOLD 500 PACE)
SWIM:	DOWN EZ 200 STROKE

The only way to swim fast is to *SwimFAST!*

103. Mastering

SWIM:	500 YDS 2 STROKES AND DRILLS	
KICK:	2 X	(50 FLY +
		100 BK +
		150 BR +
		200 F/S)
	ON 9:00	
DRILL:	100 BK	
PULL:	8 X 100 F/S ON 1:30	
	BREATHE 5	
SWIM:	2 X 400 F/S ON 5:45	
SPRINT:	4 X 50 STROKE ON 1:15	
SWIM:	SWIM DOWN EZ 200	

19.Mastering

SWIM: 500 YDS EZ CHOICE
SWIM: 12 X 25 F/S ON :25
PULL: 2 X 300 F/S, *BREATHE 3,5,7 PER 100 ON 4:45*
KICK : 4 X 200 ON 4 :10 IM ORDER
SWIM: 6 X (100 F/S + 100 IM + 100 STROKE) ON 5:00
SPRINT: 6 X 50 F/S - 3 ON :40, 3 ON :45
SWIM: DOWN EZ 200

19.Mastering

SWIM: 500 YDS EZ CHOICE
SWIM: 12 X 25 F/S ON :25
PULL: 2 X 300 F/S, *BREATHE 3,5,7 PER 100 ON 4:45*
KICK : 4 X 200 ON 4 :10 IM ORDER
SWIM: 6 X (100 F/S + 100 IM + 100 STROKE) ON 5:00
SPRINT: 6 X 50 F/S - 3 ON :40, 3 ON :45
SWIM: DOWN EZ 200

As a nation we are dedicated to keeping physically fit and parking as close to the stadium as possible.
Bill Vaughn

104. Mastering

SWIM:	500 YDS EZ F/S WARM UP
SWIM:	10 X 50 F/S AND STROKE ALTERNATELY ON 1:00
KICK:	8 X 100 IM ON 2:00
DRILL:	8 X 25 FLY ON :30
PULL:	4 X (150 F/S + 50 BR) ON 3:30
SWIM:	2 X 150 F/S ON 2:00 2 X 75 F/S ON 1:00 2 X 25 F/S ON :20
SWIM:	800 IM *MODERATE SPEEDFOR TECHNIQUE.* *REST 5 SEC AFTER EACH FLY .*
SPRINT:	6 X 50 F/S ON :55 HOLD :36
SWIM:	DOWN EZ 200 CHOICE

20.Mastering

SWIM:	500 YDS EZ F/S AND 1 STROKE
PULL:	4 X (50 FLY + 100 F/S + 50 BR) ON 3:45
SWIM:	8 X (25 BK+ 25 BR) ON 1:00
SWIM:	3 X 400 IM ON 7:00 DESCEND
KICK:	6 X 100 IM ON 2:00
DRILL:	100 BK
SWIM:	8 X (25 BR + 25 F/S) ON 1:00
SWIM:	4 X 25 STROKE ON :30 FLY.
SPRINT:	4 X 25 STROKE ON :45 FAST
SWIM:	DOWN EZ 200 F/S

20.Mastering

SWIM:	500 YDS EZ F/S AND 1 STROKE
PULL:	4 X (50 FLY + 100 F/S + 50 BR) ON 3:45
SWIM:	8 X (25 BK+ 25 BR) ON 1:00
SWIM:	3 X 400 IM ON 7:00 DESCEND
KICK:	6 X 100 IM ON 2:00
DRILL:	100 BK
SWIM:	8 X (25 BR + 25 F/S) ON 1:00
SWIM:	4 X 25 STROKE ON :30 FLY.
SPRINT:	4 X 25 STROKE ON :45 FAST
SWIM:	DOWN EZ 200 F/S

Don't count the days; make the days count.

105. Mastering

SWIM:	500 YDS F/S AND STROKE EZ WARM UP
KICK:	2 X (3 X 100) ALTERNATE FLY, BK, BR ON 2:00
DRILL:	200 IM
PULL:	8 X (75 F/S + 25 STROKE) ON 1:45
SWIM:	10 X 75 F/S ON 1:00 (500 PACE)
SWIM:	6 X 100 IM, 3 ON 1:45, 3 ON 2:00 (HOLD 1:25)
SWIM:	400 F/S *FOR FEEL AND TECHNIQUE ON 6:15*
SWIM:	SWIM DOWN EZ 200

21. Mastering

SWIM:	500 YDS EZ CHOICE
KICK:	8 X 50 ON 1:00, 2 EACH STROKE
PULL:	6 X 100 F/S ON 1:30, *BREATHE 4 & 6 PER 50*
SWIM:	4 X 200 STROKE ON 3:30 (NO F/S)
DRILL:	200 2ND BEST STROKE (NO F/S)
SWIM:	4 X 100 ON 2:00, 2ND BEST STROKE
SWIM:	12 X 75 F/S AS 3 ON 1:00, 4 ON 1:05, 5 ON 1:10
SPRINT:	4 X 25 F/S ON :30 (HOLD :15)
SWIM:	DOWN EZ 200 STROKE

21. Mastering

SWIM:	500 YDS EZ CHOICE
KICK:	8 X 50 ON 1:00, 2 EACH STROKE
PULL:	6 X 100 F/S ON 1:30, *BREATHE 4 & 6 PER 50*
SWIM:	4 X 200 STROKE ON 3:30 (NO F/S)
DRILL:	200 2ND BEST STROKE (NO F/S)
SWIM:	4 X 100 ON 2:00, 2ND BEST STROKE
SWIM:	12 X 75 F/S AS 3 ON 1:00, 4 ON 1:05, 5 ON 1:10
SPRINT:	4 X 25 F/S ON :30 (HOLD :15)
SWIM:	DOWN EZ 200 STROKE

Don't postpone joy.

106. Mastering

SWIM:	500 YDS F/S EZ USE DRILLS	
KICK:	8 X (50 F/S + 25 STROKE) ON 1:30	
DRILL:	4 X 25 BK ON :30	
SWIM:	8 X 50 F/S ON :50	
	DESCEND FROM :43 TO :36	
PULL:	6 X (25 FLY + 100 F/S + 25 BR) ON 2:30	
SWIM:	4 X	(50 FLY + 50 BK ON 1:45
		(50 BK + 50 BR ON 1:45
		(50 BR + 50 F/S ON 1:45
		(100 F/S ON 1:30)
SWIM:	SWIM DOWN EZ 200 CHOICE	

22. Mastering

SWIM:	500 YDS F/S WARM-UP
SWIM:	10 X 75 F/S ON 1:10 (HOLD :59)
KICK:	5 X 100 ON 2:00 IM AND F/S
DRILL:	100 IM REVERSE ORDER
SWIM:	4 X (200 IM ON 3:30 + 100 F/S ON 1:30)
PULL:	(100 F/S *BREATHE 7* + 5 SEC + 200 F/S *BREATHE 5* + 10 SEC + 300 F/S *BREATHE 3*)
SPRINT:	12 X 25, 3 EACH STROKE IM ORDER ON :30
SWIM:	DOWN EZ 200 F/S

22. Mastering

SWIM:	500 YDS F/S WARM-UP
SWIM:	10 X 75 F/S ON 1:10 (HOLD :59)
KICK:	5 X 100 ON 2:00 IM AND F/S
DRILL:	100 IM REVERSE ORDER
SWIM:	4 X (200 IM ON 3:30 + 100 F/S ON 1:30)
PULL:	(100 F/S *BREATHE 7* + 5 SEC + 200 F/S *BREATHE 5* + 10 SEC + 300 F/S *BREATHE 3*)
SPRINT:	12 X 25, 3 EACH STROKE IM ORDER ON :30
SWIM:	DOWN EZ 200 F/S

Everything that is, is within.

107. Mastering

SWIM:	500 YDS EZ CHOICE	
SWIM:	8 X 50 F/S ON :40	
	REPEAT FAILURES !	
PULL:	800 F/S WITH EACH 4TH 50 STROKE	
KICK:	6 X 100 ALTERNATE BR AND F/S ON 2:00	
DRILL:	100 BR	
SWIM:	2 X	(2 X 150 F/S ON 2:05
		(2 X 75 F/S ON 1:00
		(2 X 25 F/S ON :25)
DRILL:	4 X 25 IM ORDER ON :30	
SPRINT:	4 X 100 STROKE ON 2:00	
SWIM:	DOWN EZ 200 F/S	

23. Mastering

SWIM: 500 YDS EZ WARM-UP ALL STROKES
KICK: 10 X 50 ALTERNATE F/S AND CHOICE ON 1:00
PULL: 3 X (150 F/S + 50 BR) ON 3:30
SWIM: 200 STROKE *(FOR TECHNIQUE)*
SWIM: 800 IM (i.e. 4 X 200)
SWIM: 200 2ND STROKE *(FOR TECHNIQUE)*
SWIM: 10 X (25 FLY + 25 BK) ON 1:00
10 X (25 BK + 25 BR) ON :55
10 X (25 BR + 25 F/S) ON :50
SWIM: DOWN EZ 200 F/S

23. Mastering

SWIM: 500 YDS EZ WARM-UP ALL STROKES
KICK: 10 X 50 ALTERNATE F/S AND CHOICE ON 1:00
PULL: 3 X (150 F/S + 50 BR) ON 3:30
SWIM: 200 STROKE *(FOR TECHNIQUE)*
SWIM: 800 IM (i.e. 4 X 200)
SWIM: 200 2ND STROKE *(FOR TECHNIQUE)*
SWIM: 10 X (25 FLY + 25 BK) ON 1:00
10 X (25 BK + 25 BR) ON :55
10 X (25 BR + 25 F/S) ON :50
SWIM: DOWN EZ 200 F/S

You can't swim fast in meets by swimming slow in practice.

108. Mastering

SWIM:	500 YDS F/S EZ AND LONG
SWIM:	5 X 100 F/S ON 1:45 HOLD 1:15
KICK:	10 X 50 CHOICE ON 1:00
DRILL:	6 X 25 FLY ON :30
PULL:	10 X (25 STROKE + 75 F/S) ON 1:45
SWIM:	4 X 200 IM ON 4:00 HOLD 3 :10
SPRINT:	8 X 30 YDS F/S FAST IN AND OUT OF TURNS ON 1:15
SWIM:	DOWN EZ 200 STROKE

24. Mastering

SWIM:	500 YDS EZ F/S WARM-UP
SWIM:	8 X (25 FLY + 25 F/S + 25 FLY) ON 1:30
KICK:	25 EZ + 25 FAST FOR 500 YDS F/S
DRILL:	100 IM
PULL:	12 X 75 F/S ON 1:15 *BREATHE 2,4,6 PER 25*
SWIM:	3 X 600 F/S ON 9:00 DESCEND TIME
SPRINT:	8 X 25 ON :30, ALTERNATE IM ORDER STROKE AND F/S
SWIM:	DOWN EZ 200 CHOICE

24. Mastering

SWIM:	500 YDS EZ F/S WARM-UP
SWIM:	8 X (25 FLY + 25 F/S + 25 FLY) ON 1:30
KICK:	25 EZ + 25 FAST FOR 500 YDS F/S
DRILL:	100 IM
PULL:	12 X 75 F/S ON 1:15 *BREATHE 2,4,6 PER 25*
SWIM:	3 X 600 F/S ON 9:00 DESCEND TIME
SPRINT:	8 X 25 ON :30, ALTERNATE IM ORDER STROKE AND F/S
SWIM:	DOWN EZ 200 CHOICE

If you're happy, notify your face.

109. Mastering

SWIM:	500 YDS USE F/S AND 1 STROKE EZ
SWIM:	8 X 50 F/S ON :40 (PACE)
KICK:	600 IM (150 EACH STROKE) ON 13:00
DRILL:	4 X 50 IM ON 1:00
SWIM:	8 X (25 FLY + 75 BK) ON 1:50
PULL:	200 BR + 300 F/S ON 8:30
SWIM:	800 F/S BUILD EACH 200 - *GOOD TECHNIQUE THROUGHOUT* ON 11:30
SPRINT:	6 X 75 F/S ON 1:20 HOLD :59
SWIM:	DOWN EZ 200 F/S

25. Mastering

SWIM:	500 YDS EZ F/S AND 1 STROKE
SWIM:	4 X 125 STROKE ON 2:15
KICK:	10 X 50 ALTERNATE F/S AND CHOICE ON 1:00
DRILL:	100 REVERSE IM
PULL:	6 X 150 F/S ON 2:10 *BREATHE 4*
SWIM:	3 X 500 F/S ON 7:15 DESCEND
SWIM:	DOWN EZ 200 STROKE

25. Mastering

SWIM:	500 YDS EZ F/S AND 1 STROKE
SWIM:	4 X 125 STROKE ON 2:15
KICK:	10 X 50 ALTERNATE F/S AND CHOICE ON 1:00
DRILL:	100 REVERSE IM
PULL:	6 X 150 F/S ON 2:10 *BREATHE 4*
SWIM:	3 X 500 F/S ON 7:15 DESCEND
SWIM:	DOWN EZ 200 STROKE

Work = yardage x intensity.
Dick Jochums

110. Mastering

SWIM:	500 YDS ALL STROKES EZ
SWIM:	100 F/S ON 1:30
	200 F/S ON 3:00
	300 F/S ON 4:30
	400 F/S ON 5:45
	300 F/S ON 4:15
	200 F/S ON 2:45
	100 F/S FAST
KICK:	6 X 100
	ALTERNATE F/S AND STROKE
	ON 2:00
DRILL:	100 F/S CATCH-UP DRILL
PULL:	6 X (50 CHOICE + 50 F/S) ON 2:00
SPRINT:	8 X 50 1ST STROKE ON 1:15
SWIM:	DOWN EZ 200 STROKE

26. Mastering

SWIM: 500 YDS EZ CHOICE
KICK: 5 X 100 IM ON 2:00
SWIM: 8 X 100 IM AS
4 ON 1:40,
4 ON 1:45
KICK: 8 X 25 ALTERNATE BR AND F/S
ON :30
PULL: 18 X 50 F/S AS
6 ON :45,
6 ON :50,
6 ON :55
SWIM: 4 X (25 FLY + 125 STROKE + 25 F/S)
ON 3:15
SWIM: DOWN EZ 200 F/S

26. Mastering

SWIM: 500 YDS EZ CHOICE
KICK: 5 X 100 IM ON 2:00
SWIM: 8 X 100 IM AS
4 ON 1:40,
4 ON 1:45
KICK: 8 X 25 ALTERNATE BR AND F/S
ON :30
PULL: 18 X 50 F/S AS
6 ON :45,
6 ON :50,
6 ON :55
SWIM: 4 X (25 FLY + 125 STROKE + 25 F/S)
ON 3:15
SWIM: DOWN EZ 200 F/S

Winning isn't the most important thing, but trying to win is.

111. Mastering

SWIM:	500 YDS WARM UP	
KICK:	6 X 100 IM ON 2:00	
DRILL:	100 IM	
SWIM:	3 X	(150 F/S ON 2:10
		(2 X 100 F/S ON 1:30
		(4 X 50 F/S ON :45)
PULL:	2 X (100 F/S + 100 STROKE) ON 3:30	
SWIM:	2 X	(75 STROKE ON 1:20
		(2 X 50 STROKE ON :55
		(4 X 25 STROKE ON :30)
SWIM:	DOWN EZ 200 F/S	

27. Mastering

SWIM:	500 YDS EZ WARM-UP
KICK:	2 X 250 FLY AND BR ON 5:00
SWIM:	8 X 50 F/S ON :45 (HOLD :39)
SWIM:	6 X (25 FLY + 50 F/S + 50 BR) ON 2:00
DRILL:	200 IM REVERSE ORDER
SWIM:	4 X (3 X 100 AS 50 FLY/50 BK, 50 BK/50 BR, 50 BR/50 F/S) *ALL ABOVE ON 2:00 WITH NO REST BREAK BETWEEN SETS*
SWIM:	200 IM FOR TIME
SWIM:	DOWN EZ 300 STROKE

27. Mastering

SWIM:	500 YDS EZ WARM-UP
KICK:	2 X 250 FLY AND BR ON 5:00
SWIM:	8 X 50 F/S ON :45 (HOLD :39)
SWIM:	6 X (25 FLY + 50 F/S + 50 BR) ON 2:00
DRILL:	200 IM REVERSE ORDER
SWIM:	4 X (3 X 100 AS 50 FLY/50 BK, 50 BK/50 BR, 50 BR/50 F/S) *ALL ABOVE ON 2:00 WITH NO REST BREAK BETWEEN SETS*
SWIM:	200 IM FOR TIME
SWIM:	DOWN EZ 300 STROKE

Design a workout that even a fool could use, and only a fool will use it.

112. Mastering

SWIM:	800 F/S WARM UP
SWIM:	10 X 50 F/S ON 1:00 HOLD :36
KICK:	6 X 100 ON 2:00 USE ALL 4 STROKES
DRILL:	8 X 25 FLY ON :30
SWIM:	5 X 100 F/S ON 1:20 (PACE)
PULL:	400 FLY BK OR BR
SWIM:	6 X 100 IM ON 2:00 (HOLD SUB 1:30)
SWIM:	4 X 50 F/S ON :50 HOLD :35
SWIM:	DOWN EZ 200 STROKE

28. Mastering

SWIM:	500 YDS EZ ALL 4 STROKES
PULL:	6 X (125 F/S + 25 BR) ON 2:30
DRILL:	200 CHOICE
SWIM:	16 X 25 F/S ON :25
KICK:	10 X 50 ON 1:00
	USE 2 DIFFERENT STROKES
SWIM:	8 X 100 F/S ON 1:30 (HOLD 1:19)
SWIM:	200 BEST STROKE (NOT F/S)
SWIM:	8 X 50 ON 1:00 WORST STROKE
SPRINT:	4 X 25 F/S ON :40
	BREATHE TWICE PER 25
SWIM:	DOWN EZ 200 F/S

28. Mastering

SWIM:	500 YDS EZ ALL 4 STROKES
PULL:	6 X (125 F/S + 25 BR) ON 2:30
DRILL:	200 CHOICE
SWIM:	16 X 25 F/S ON :25
KICK:	10 X 50 ON 1:00
	USE 2 DIFFERENT STROKES
SWIM:	8 X 100 F/S ON 1:30 (HOLD 1:19)
SWIM:	200 BEST STROKE (NOT F/S)
SWIM:	8 X 50 ON 1:00 WORST STROKE
SPRINT:	4 X 25 F/S ON :40
	BREATHE TWICE PER 25
SWIM:	DOWN EZ 200 F/S

One old swim coach tried to trick an other: "If you can tell me how many chickens I have in this sack, I'll give you both of them."

113. Mastering

SWIM:	600 YDS USING 3 STROKES EZ
SWIM:	16 X 25 F/S ON :30 HOLD:19
KICK:	16 X 50 ON 1:00
	ALTERNATE F/S AND CHOICE
PULL:	5 X (50 STROKE + 150 F/S) ON 3:30
SWIM:	4 X (75 FLY + 50 BK) ON 2:15
SWIM:	8 X (50 BK + 50 BR) ON 1:50
SWIM:	DOWN EZ 200 F/S

29. Mastering

SWIM:	500 YDS EZ F/S
SWIM:	100 FLY + 100 BK ON 3:45
	100 BK + 100 BR ON 3:45
	100 BR + 100 F/S ON 3:45
KICK:	3 X 200 IM ON 4:15 DESCEND
PULL:	75, 100, 125, 100, 75 F/S WITH
	5 SEC REST
SWIM:	8 X 100 STROKE ON 1:50
SWIM:	2 X 200 ANOTHER STROKE ON 3:45
SWIM:	16 X 25 ON :30
	ALTERNATE FLY AND F/S
SWIM:	DOWN EZ 200 STROKE

29. Mastering

SWIM:	500 YDS EZ F/S
SWIM:	100 FLY + 100 BK ON 3:45
	100 BK + 100 BR ON 3:45
	100 BR + 100 F/S ON 3:45
KICK:	3 X 200 IM ON 4:15 DESCEND
PULL:	75, 100, 125, 100, 75 F/S WITH
	5 SEC REST
SWIM:	8 X 100 STROKE ON 1:50
SWIM:	2 X 200 ANOTHER STROKE ON 3:45
SWIM:	16 X 25 ON :30
	ALTERNATE FLY AND F/S
SWIM:	DOWN EZ 200 STROKE

Hurt. Pain. Agony.

Dr. James Counsilman

114. Mastering

SWIM:	600 YDS F/S AND 1 STROKE EZ
KICK:	400 IM ON 8:00
PULL:	6 X (50 BR + 150 F/S) ON 3:30
SWIM:	6 X 25 FLY ON :30 HOLD :22
SWIM:	6 X (25 FLY + 25 BK) ON 1:00 HOLD :49
SWIM:	6 X (25 FLY + 25 BK +25 BR) ON 1:30 HOLD 1:15
SWIM:	6 X 100 IM ON 2:00 HOLD 1:25
DRILL:	400 IM
SWIM:	DOWN EZ 200 CHOICE

30. Mastering

SWIM:	500 YDS EZ 2 STROKES
KICK:	4 X 100 IM ORDER ON 2:00
KICK:	8 X 50 ALTERNATE F/S AND STROKE ON 1:00
DRILL:	100 CHOICE
PULL:	5 X 200 F/S ON 3:15 *BREATHE 5,7 PER 100*
SWIM:	400 IM ON 6:30
	2 X 200 IM ON 3:30
	4 X 100 IM ON 1:45
SPRINT:	8 X 25 ALTERNATE F/S AND FLY ON :30
SWIM:	DOWN EZ 200 CHOICE

30. Mastering

SWIM:	500 YDS EZ 2 STROKES
KICK:	4 X 100 IM ORDER ON 2:00
KICK:	8 X 50 ALTERNATE F/S AND STROKE ON 1:00
DRILL:	100 CHOICE
PULL:	5 X 200 F/S ON 3:15 *BREATHE 5,7 PER 100*
SWIM:	400 IM ON 6:30
	2 X 200 IM ON 3:30
	4 X 100 IM ON 1:45
SPRINT:	8 X 25 ALTERNATE F/S AND FLY ON :30
SWIM:	DOWN EZ 200 CHOICE

Learn to love water.

115. Mastering

SWIM:	500 YDS F/S WARM UP EZ
KICK:	8 X 25 F/S ON :25 *REST :30*
	8 X 25 CHOICE ON :25 *REST :30*
	8 X 25 F/S ON :25
SWIM:	8 X 75 F/S ON 1:00 (500 PACE)
SWIM:	6 X 50 BK ON 1:00
PULL:	4 X 225 F/S ON 3:15
SWIM:	18 X 50 ON 1:00
	ALTERNATE FLY,BK,BR
SWIM:	4 X 50 F/S ON :40 HOLD :36
SWIM:	DOWN 200 STROKE

31. Mastering

SWIM: 500 YDS F/S EZ
SWIM: 8 X 25 FLY ON :30
KICK: 8 X 75 ON 1:30 , 2 EACH STROKE
DRILL: 200 IM
PULL: 6 X 100 ON 2:00, 2 BK, 2 BR, 2 F/S
SWIM: 5 X (3 X 50 F/S ON:50,
1 X 50 FLY ON :50)
KICK: 100 IM
SPRINT: 4 X 50 BK ON 1:00
4 X 50 BR ON 1:00
SWIM: DOWN EZ 200 F/S

31. Mastering

SWIM: 500 YDS F/S EZ
SWIM: 8 X 25 FLY ON :30
KICK: 8 X 75 ON 1:30 , 2 EACH STROKE
DRILL: 200 IM
PULL: 6 X 100 ON 2:00, 2 BK, 2 BR, 2 F/S
SWIM: 5 X (3 X 50 F/S ON:50,
1 X 50 FLY ON :50)
KICK: 100 IM
SPRINT: 4 X 50 BK ON 1:00
4 X 50 BR ON 1:00
SWIM: DOWN EZ 200 F/S

What the caterpillar thinks is the end of life, the butterfly knows is the beginning.

116. Mastering

SWIM:	500 YDS CHOICE OF 2 STROKES EZ
SWIM:	8 X 75 F/S ON 1:15 HOLD :56
KICK:	8 X 100 ON 2:00 IM ORDER
PULL:	800 F/S ON 11:45
SWIM:	3 X 200 BR OR IM ON 3:45
	3 X 200 FLY OR BK ON 3:45
SPRINT:	4 X 50 IM ORDER ON 1:00
SWIM:	DOWN EZ 200 F/S

32. Mastering

SWIM:	500 YDS EZ
SWIM:	5 X (200 F/S, 5 SEC REST)
KICK:	10 X 50 ALTERNATE F/S AND CHOICE ON 1:00
SWIM:	4 X 125 F/S ON 1:45
	4 X 75 F/S ON 1:05
	4 X 50 F/S ON :40
PULL:	6 X (50 F/S + 50 BR) ON 2:00
SPRINT:	4 X 25 STROKE ON :30
	4 X 25 F/S ON :25
SWIM:	DOWN EZ 200 CHOICE

32. Mastering

SWIM:	500 YDS EZ
SWIM:	5 X (200 F/S, 5 SEC REST)
KICK:	10 X 50 ALTERNATE F/S AND CHOICE ON 1:00
SWIM:	4 X 125 F/S ON 1:45
	4 X 75 F/S ON 1:05
	4 X 50 F/S ON :40
PULL:	6 X (50 F/S + 50 BR) ON 2:00
SPRINT:	4 X 25 STROKE ON :30
	4 X 25 F/S ON :25
SWIM:	DOWN EZ 200 CHOICE

What the caterpillar thinks is the end of life, the butterfly knows is the beginning.

117. Mastering

SWIM:	500 YDS F/S AND DRILLS EZ
SWIM:	20 X 25 F/S ON :25
KICK:	600 IM ON 12:30
PULL:	6 X 50 BR ON 1:10
KICK:	8 X 25 FLY ON :25
PULL:	6 X (25 STROKE + 100 F/S) ON 2:00
SWIM:	4 X (200 IM + 50 STROKE) ON 4 :15
SWIM:	1 X 200 F/S FOR TIME (95% EFFORT)
SWIM:	DOWN EZ 200 F/S

33. Mastering

SWIM:	500 YDS EZ USE 3 STROKES
KICK:	4 X 150 IM ORDER ON 3:00
SWIM:	6 X (25 FLY + 100 BK) ON 2 :15
PULL:	6 X (50 STROKE + 50 F/S) ON 1:45
SWIM:	6 X (50 BR + 75 F/S) ON 2 :15
SWIM:	20 X 25 IN 4 SETS OF 5 ALTERNATE 4 BK, 4 F/S ON :30
SWIM:	DOWN 200 STROKE

33. Mastering

SWIM:	500 YDS EZ USE 3 STROKES
KICK:	4 X 150 IM ORDER ON 3:00
SWIM:	6 X (25 FLY + 100 BK) ON 2 :15
PULL:	6 X (50 STROKE + 50 F/S) ON 1:45
SWIM:	6 X (50 BR + 75 F/S) ON 2 :15
SWIM:	20 X 25 IN 4 SETS OF 5 ALTERNATE 4 BK, 4 F/S ON :30
SWIM:	DOWN 200 STROKE

You're not old until it takes you longer to rest up than it does to get tired. *Dr. Phong Allen*

118. Mastering

SWIM:	500 YDS ALL 4 STROKES EZ
SWIM:	8 X 50 F/S ALTERNATE ON :40 AND :45
KICK:	12 X 50 IM ORDER ON 1:00
PULL:	3 X 300 F/S ON 4:20
SWIM:	4 X 100 IM ON 1:45
SWIM:	8 X 25 BR ON :30
SWIM:	4 X 100 F/S ON 1:45 HOLD 1:15
SWIM:	4 X 100 BK ON 2:00
SPRINT:	4 X 25 F/S ON :30
	4 X 25 F/S ON :25
	4 X 25 F/S ON :20
	REST 20 SEC BETWEEN SETS
SWIM:	DOWN EZ 200 F/S

34. Mastering

SWIM:	500 YDS EZ F/S
	(DRILL 50/SWIM 50) FOR 400 IM
KICK:	16 X 25 IM ORDER ON :30
DRILL:	100 F/S
SWIM:	6 X (100 BK + 25 BR) ON 2:15
PULL:	6 X (25 FLY + 50 BK + 25 BR + 50 F/S) ON 2:45
SWIM:	4 X 200 F/S ON 2:50 HOLD 2:44
SPRINT:	8 X 25 FLY ON :30
SWIM:	DOWN EZ 200 F/S

34. Mastering

SWIM:	500 YDS EZ F/S
	(DRILL 50/SWIM 50) FOR 400 IM
KICK:	16 X 25 IM ORDER ON :30
DRILL:	100 F/S
SWIM:	6 X (100 BK + 25 BR) ON 2:15
PULL:	6 X (25 FLY + 50 BK + 25 BR + 50 F/S) ON 2:45
SWIM:	4 X 200 F/S ON 2:50 HOLD 2:44
SPRINT:	8 X 25 FLY ON :30
SWIM:	DOWN EZ 200 F/S

The thrill comes in doing your best time, something you haven't done before. *John Haber*

119. Mastering

SWIM:	500 YDS EZ F/S WARM UP
SWIM:	4 X 150 F/S ON 2 :10 HOLD 1:55
KICK:	400 REVERSE IM
SWIM:	6 X (25 FLY + 100 BK) ON 2 :15
PULL:	3 X (300 F/S + 50 BR) ON 5:45
SWIM:	3 X 200 IM ON 3:45 HOLD 3:05
SPRINT:	4 X 50 F/S ON 1:15 HOLD :36
SWIM:	DOWN EZ 200 CHOICE

35. Mastering

SWIM:	500 YDS EZ CHOICE
KICK:	10 X 50 ALTERNATE BR AND F/S ON 1:00
DRILL:	200 BK
SWIM:	6 X 50 BK ON 1:00
PULL:	6 X 100 F/S ON 1:25
SWIM:	12 X 75 F/S ON 1:05
DRILL:	200 BR
SWIM:	6 X 50 BR ON 1:00
SPRINT:	6 X 50 F/S ON :45
SWIM:	DOWN EZ 200 STROKE

35. Mastering

SWIM:	500 YDS EZ CHOICE
KICK:	10 X 50 ALTERNATE BR AND F/S ON 1:00
DRILL:	200 BK
SWIM:	6 X 50 BK ON 1:00
PULL:	6 X 100 F/S ON 1:25
SWIM:	12 X 75 F/S ON 1:05
DRILL:	200 BR
SWIM:	6 X 50 BR ON 1:00
SPRINT:	6 X 50 F/S ON :45
SWIM:	DOWN EZ 200 STROKE

The thrill comes in doing your best time, something you haven't done before. *John Haber*

120. Mastering

SWIM:	500 YDS STROKES AND DRILLS EZ
SWIM:	20 X 25 F/S ON :40 HOLD :17
KICK:	4 X 150 CHOICE ON 2:55
PULL:	800 F/S
	BREATHE 3,5 PER ALTERNATE 100
SWIM:	4 X (100 FLY + 25 BK + 25 BR) ON 2:30
	4 X (100 BK + 25 BR + 25 F/S) ON 2:30
	4 X (100 BR + 25 F/S) ON 2 :15
	4 X 100 F/S ON 1:45
SWIM:	DOWN EZ 200 F/S

36. Mastering

SWIM:	500 YDS EZ WARM-UP CHOICE
SWIM:	16 X 25 F/S ON :20
KICK:	200 IM + 6 X 50 BK, BR ON 1:00
PULL:	2 X (300 F/S + 50 STROKE) ON 5:25
SWIM:	4 X 300 IM - OMIT FLY, BK, BR AND F/S LEGS ON 1,2,3,4 RESPECTIVELY ON 5:15
SWIM:	4 X 100 BK ON 2:00
SPRINT:	4 X 25 F/S ON :30 *NO BREATHE*
SWIM:	DOWN EZ 200 F/S

36. Mastering

SWIM:	500 YDS EZ WARM-UP CHOICE
SWIM:	16 X 25 F/S ON :20
KICK:	200 IM + 6 X 50 BK, BR ON 1:00
PULL:	2 X (300 F/S + 50 STROKE) ON 5:25
SWIM:	4 X 300 IM - OMIT FLY, BK, BR AND F/S LEGS ON 1,2,3,4 RESPECTIVELY ON 5:15
SWIM:	4 X 100 BK ON 2:00
SPRINT:	4 X 25 F/S ON :30 *NO BREATHE*
SWIM:	DOWN EZ 200 F/S

The only way to win is to work at it. *Earl Anthony*

121. Mastering

SWIM:	500 YDS EZ WARM UP
KICK:	150 EACH STROKE IM ORDER ON 3:00
KICK:	4 X 50 FLY ON 1:00
PULL:	500 F/S ON 7:00 *BREATHE EVERY 5*
PULL:	6 X 50 STROKE ON 1:00
SWIM:	20 X 50 F/S 10 ON :40, 10 ON :45
SWIM:	10 X 50 STROKE (FAST) ON 1:15
SWIM:	10 X 25 F/S ON :20 HOLD :15
SWIM:	DOWN EZ 200 F/S

37. Mastering

SWIM:	500 YDS EZ F/S AND STROKE
SWIM:	4 X (25 FLY + 25 BK) ON :55
	4 X (25 BK + 25 BR) ON :55
	4 X (25 BR + 25 F/S) ON :55
KICK:	200 BR ON 4:00
	4 X 50 BK ON 1:00
	4 X 50 FLY ON 1:00
DRILL:	200 IM REVERSE ORDER
SWIM:	8 X 150 F/S, 4 ON 2:10, 4 ON 2:15
KICK:	16 X 25 F/S ALTERNATE ON :25 AND :30
SWIM:	2 X (4 X 75 IM) ON 5:00 DESCEND
SWIM:	DOWN EZ 200 CHOICE

37. Mastering

SWIM:	500 YDS EZ F/S AND STROKE
SWIM:	4 X (25 FLY + 25 BK) ON :55
	4 X (25 BK + 25 BR) ON :55
	4 X (25 BR + 25 F/S) ON :55
KICK:	200 BR ON 4:00
	4 X 50 BK ON 1:00
	4 X 50 FLY ON 1:00
DRILL:	200 IM REVERSE ORDER
SWIM:	8 X 150 F/S, 4 ON 2:10, 4 ON 2:15
KICK:	16 X 25 F/S ALTERNATE ON :25 AND :30
SWIM:	2 X (4 X 75 IM) ON 5:00 DESCEND
SWIM:	DOWN EZ 200 CHOICE

You are the only one who can use your ability. It is an awesome responsibility.

122. Mastering

SWIM:	500 YDS USING F/S AND STROKES
SWIM :	8 X 75 F/S ON 1:00 (500 PACE)
KICK:	6 X 100 ALTERNATE FLY-ON-BACK, F/S EVERY 2:00
SWIM:	8 X 50 ON 1:10 IM ORDER
SWIM:	8 X 50 F/S ON 1:00 HOLD :39
PULL:	4 X (100 F/S + 25 BR) ON 2:00
SWIM:	6 X 100 IM ON 1:40 HOLD 1:28
SWIM:	8 X (25 F/S + TURN FAST) ON 1:00
SWIM:	DOWN EZ 200 F/S

38. Mastering

SWIM:	500 YDS EZ CHOICE
SWIM:	30 X 25 F/S WITH EACH 5TH FLY ON :30
KICK:	4 X 100 IM ORDER ON 2:00
SWIM:	8 X 100 STROKE ON 1:50 (DRILL 100, KICK 100) CHOICE
PULL:	2 X (200 F/S + 50 BR) ON 4:00
SWIM:	8 X (100 F/S + 5 SEC + 25 STROKE) ON 2:00
SWIM:	DOWN EZ 200 F/S

38. Mastering

SWIM:	500 YDS EZ CHOICE
SWIM:	30 X 25 F/S WITH EACH 5TH FLY ON :30
KICK:	4 X 100 IM ORDER ON 2:00
SWIM:	8 X 100 STROKE ON 1:50 (DRILL 100, KICK 100) CHOICE
PULL:	2 X (200 F/S + 50 BR) ON 4:00
SWIM:	8 X (100 F/S + 5 SEC + 25 STROKE) ON 2:00
SWIM:	DOWN EZ 200 F/S

What is the difference between ignorance and apathy? I don't know and I don't care!

123. Mastering

SWIM:	500 YDS ALL STROKES EZ
SWIM:	1, 000 YDS ON 14:30 CHECK 800 TIME
SWIM:	800 YDS FASTER THAN PREVIOUS 800. CHECK 600 TIME.
SWIM:	600 YDS FASTER THAN PREVIOUS 600. CHECK 400 TIME.
SWIM:	400 YDS FASTER THAN PREVIOUS 400. CHECK 200 TIME.
SWIM:	200 YDS FASTER THAN PREVIOUS 200.
KICK:	5 X (75 STROKE + 25 F/S) ON 2:05
SWIM:	DOWN EZ 200

39. Mastering

SWIM:	500 YDS EZ F/S WARM-UP
KICK:	200 BR + 200 F/S ON 8:00
SWIM:	500 F/S *EASY PACE FOR TECHNIQUE*
KICK:	12 X 25 ALTERNATE FLY AND F/S ON :30
DRILL:	4 X 50 FLY ON 1:00
SWIM:	8 X (25 FLY + 25 BK + 25 BR) ON 1:30 HOLDING 1:10
PULL:	3 X 200 F/S ON 3:00 *BREATHE 5*
SWIM:	8 X 50 BEST STROKE ON 1:00 8 X 50 WORST STROKE ON 1:15
SPRINT:	4 X 25 F/S ON :40 *NO BREATHE*
SWIM:	DOWN EZ 200 STROKE

39. Mastering

SWIM:	500 YDS EZ F/S WARM-UP
KICK:	200 BR + 200 F/S ON 8:00
SWIM:	500 F/S *EASY PACE FOR TECHNIQUE*
KICK:	12 X 25 ALTERNATE FLY AND F/S ON :30
DRILL:	4 X 50 FLY ON 1:00
SWIM:	8 X (25 FLY + 25 BK + 25 BR) ON 1:30 HOLDING 1:10
PULL:	3 X 200 F/S ON 3:00 *BREATHE 5*
SWIM:	8 X 50 BEST STROKE ON 1:00 8 X 50 WORST STROKE ON 1:15
SPRINT:	4 X 25 F/S ON :40 *NO BREATHE*
SWIM:	DOWN EZ 200 STROKE

Training is everything: the peach was once a bitter almond; cauliflower is nothing but cabbage with a college education.

124. Mastering

SWIM:	500 YDS CHOICE WARM UP
SWIM:	4 X (50 F/S ON :45 + 25 F/S ON :25)
KICK:	12 X 50 IM ORDER ON 1:05
DRILL:	100 BK
SWIM:	8 X 50 ON 1:00
	ALTERNATE FLY & BK
PULL:	12 X (25 BR + 75 F/S) ON 1:45
SWIM:	3 X 100 BK ON 1:50
SWIM:	6 X 50 BR ON 1:00
SPRINT:	8 X (25 + FAST TURN) ON 1:15
SWIM:	DOWN EZ 200 F/S

40. Mastering

SWIM:	500 YDS EZ 2 STROKES
KICK:	8 X 100 IM ORDER ON 2:00
DRILL:	8 X 25 BK ON :30
PULL:	300 F/S ON 4:15
	200 F/S ON 3:00
	100 F/S ON 1:45
	NEGATIVE SPLIT EACH DISTANCE
SWIM:	12 X 25 FLY ON :30
	8 X 50 BK ON 1:00
	4 X 100 BR ON 2:00
	3 X 200 F/S ON 3:00
SWIM:	100 EZ STROKE
SWIM:	1 X 200 IM FOR TIME
SWIM:	DOWN EZ 200 F/S

40. Mastering

SWIM:	500 YDS EZ 2 STROKES
KICK:	8 X 100 IM ORDER ON 2:00
DRILL:	8 X 25 BK ON :30
PULL:	300 F/S ON 4:15
	200 F/S ON 3:00
	100 F/S ON 1:45
	NEGATIVE SPLIT EACH DISTANCE
SWIM:	12 X 25 FLY ON :30
	8 X 50 BK ON 1:00
	4 X 100 BR ON 2:00
	3 X 200 F/S ON 3:00
SWIM:	100 EZ STROKE
SWIM:	1 X 200 IM FOR TIME
SWIM:	DOWN EZ 200 F/S

We are what we think we are.

125. Mastering

SWIM:	500 YDS F/S EZ
SWIM:	16 X 25 IM ORDER ON :30
KICK:	8 X (50 STROKE ON 1:05 + 25 F/S ON :30)
SWIM:	4 X 50 FLY ON 1:10 DESCEND
PULL:	6 X (75 F/S + 25 STROKE) ON 1:45
SWIM:	6 X (50 FLY + 50 BK) ON 2:00
	6 X (50 BK + 50 BR) ON 2:00
	6 X (50 BR + 50 F/S) ON 2:00
SWIM:	DOWN EZ 200 CHOICE

41. Mastering

SWIM:	500 YDS F/S EZ
SWIM:	8 X 75 BK ON 1:20
KICK:	4 X 200 ON 4:00
	ALTERNATE IM AND STROKE
DRILL:	100 BK
PULL:	2 X 400 F/S ON 6:00
	BREATHE 3,5 PER 100
SWIM:	8 X 100 ON 1:45 AS:
	100 FLY, 50 FLY/50 BK,
	100 BK, 50 BK/50 BR,
	100 BR, 50 BR/50 F/S,
	100 F/S, 100 IM
SWIM:	200 BR ON 4:00 FOR STROKE
SWIM:	8 X 25 BK ON :30 *TECHNIQUE*
SPRINT:	4 X 75 F/S ON 1:20 HOLD 1:00
SWIM:	DOWN EZ 200 STROKE

41. Mastering

SWIM:	500 YDS F/S EZ
SWIM:	8 X 75 BK ON 1:20
KICK:	4 X 200 ON 4:00
	ALTERNATE IM AND STROKE
DRILL:	100 BK
PULL:	2 X 400 F/S ON 6:00
	BREATHE 3,5 PER 100
SWIM:	8 X 100 ON 1:45 AS:
	100 FLY, 50 FLY/50 BK,
	100 BK, 50 BK/50 BR,
	100 BR, 50 BR/50 F/S,
	100 F/S, 100 IM
SWIM:	200 BR ON 4:00 FOR STROKE
SWIM:	8 X 25 BK ON :30 *TECHNIQUE*
SPRINT:	4 X 75 F/S ON 1:20 HOLD 1:00
SWIM:	DOWN EZ 200 STROKE

It is your right to succeed.

126. Mastering

SWIM:	500 YDS F/S WARM UP
SWIM:	16 X 25 F/S ON :25
KICK:	8 X 75 ON 1:30 IM ORDER
PULL:	200 F/S ON 3:15
	150 F/S + 50 BR ON 3:15
	200 F/S ON 3:15
	(100 F/S + 50 BR + 50 F/S) ON 3:15
	200 F/S ON 3:15
SWIM:	6 X (25 FLY + 100 BR + 25 F/S) ON 2:45
	6 X (100 BK + 25 BR + 25 F/S) ON 2:45
SWIM:	DOWN EZ 200 CHOICE

42. Mastering

SWIM:	500 YDS EZ ALL STROKES
KICK:	10 X 50 F/S ALTERNATE SLOW/FAST ON 1:10
DRILL:	100 BK
PULL:	8 X 100 F/S ON 1:25
SWIM:	400 BK 400 BR 400 IM 400 F/S - ALL ON 7:00
SWIM:	8 X 25 ALTERNATE FLY AND F/S ON :30
SWIM:	DOWN EZ 200 F/S

42. Mastering

SWIM:	500 YDS EZ ALL STROKES
KICK:	10 X 50 F/S ALTERNATE SLOW/FAST ON 1:10
DRILL:	100 BK
PULL:	8 X 100 F/S ON 1:25
SWIM:	400 BK 400 BR 400 IM 400 F/S - ALL ON 7:00
SWIM:	8 X 25 ALTERNATE FLY AND F/S ON :30
SWIM:	DOWN EZ 200 F/S

There is only one thing in the world worse than being talked about and that is not being talked about. *Oscar Wilde*

127. Mastering

SWIM:	500 YDS CHOICE WARM UP
SWIM:	4 X 50 F/S ON :45
	8 X 25 F/S ON :25
KICK:	5 X (50 FLY + 50 F/S) ON 2:10
DRILL:	4 X 25 IM ORDER ON :30
PULL:	500 F/S EVERY 4TH LENGTH FLY,
	BREATHE EVERY 3 FOR F/S AND FLY
SWIM:	8 X (75 STROKE ON 1:30 +
	100 F/S ON 1:30)
SWIM:	4 X 100 BK ON 1:45
SWIM:	20 X 25 F/S
	ALTERNATE ON :30 AND :25
SWIM:	DOWN EZ 200 F/S

43. Mastering

SWIM:	500 YDS EZ F/S AND 1 STROKE
KICK:	8 X 75 CHOICE ON 1:30
DRILL:	200 IM
PULL:	2 X (250 F/S + 50 STROKE) ON 4:30
SWIM:	8 X 200 ON 3:45 ALTERNATE IM AND STROKE (NOT F/S)
SPRINT:	4 X 75 F/S ON 1:10 HOLD :59
SWIM:	DOWN EZ 200 CHOICE

43. Mastering

SWIM:	500 YDS EZ F/S AND 1 STROKE
KICK:	8 X 75 CHOICE ON 1:30
DRILL:	200 IM
PULL:	2 X (250 F/S + 50 STROKE) ON 4:30
SWIM:	8 X 200 ON 3:45 ALTERNATE IM AND STROKE (NOT F/S)
SPRINT:	4 X 75 F/S ON 1:10 HOLD :59
SWIM:	DOWN EZ 200 CHOICE

You need to compete for something greater than the experience of just winning.

128. Mastering

SWIM:	500 YDS F/S EZ
KICK:	6 X 100 IM ON 2:00
DRILL:	100 BR
PULL:	16 X 50 F/S ON :50
SWIM:	10 X 100 ON 2:00 AS 4 STROKE, 1 F/S, 4 STROKE, 1 F/S
DRILL:	200 BK
SPRINT:	8 X 25 F/S ON :45 *NO BREATHE LAST 10 YDS*
SWIM:	DOWN EZ 200

44. Mastering

SWIM:	500 YDS EZ WARM-UP CHOICE
SWIM:	4 X 150 F/S ON 2:15 HOLD 2:00
KICK:	5 X 100 ALTERNATE CHOICE AND F/S ON 2:00
DRILL:	4 X 25 FLY ON :30
SWIM:	3 X (250 F/S ON 3:30, 150 F/S ON 2:10, 100 F/S ON 1:25, 50 F/S ON :40) *REST :30 BETWEEN SETS*
DRILL:	100 BK
SPRINT:	8 X 25 F/S ON :30 HOLD :15
SWIM:	DOWN EZ 200 F/S

44. Mastering

SWIM:	500 YDS EZ WARM-UP CHOICE
SWIM:	4 X 150 F/S ON 2:15 HOLD 2:00
KICK:	5 X 100 ALTERNATE CHOICE AND F/S ON 2:00
DRILL:	4 X 25 FLY ON :30
SWIM:	3 X (250 F/S ON 3:30, 150 F/S ON 2:10, 100 F/S ON 1:25, 50 F/S ON :40) *REST :30 BETWEEN SETS*
DRILL:	100 BK
SPRINT:	8 X 25 F/S ON :30 HOLD :15
SWIM:	DOWN EZ 200 F/S

People who are the most effective and efficient in their fields anticipate and prepare with imagined experience.

The Pacific Institute of America

129. Mastering

SWIM:	500 YDS F/S AND STROKE WARM UP
SWIM:	8 X 50 STROKE ON :55
KICK:	24 X 25 CHOICE ON :30
DRILL:	100 REVERSE IM
SWIM:	75 F/S ON 1:00 *REST 5 SEC*
	150 F/S ON 2:00 *REST 10 SEC*
	225 F/S ON 3:00 *REST 15 SEC*
	300 F/S ON 4:00 *REST 20 SEC*
	375 F/S ON 5:00 *REST 25 SEC*
	450 F/S ON 6:00 *REST 30 SEC*
	525 F/S ON 7:00 *REST 35 SEC*
	600 F/S ON 8:00
SWIM:	DOWN EZ 200 F/S

45. Mastering

SWIM:	500 YDS WARM-UP F/S
	2 X (KICK 50/SWIM 50) FOR 400 IM
PULL:	4 X 175 F/S ON 2:45
SWIM:	10 X 50 FLY ON 1:00
	10 X 50 BK ON 1:00
	10 X 50 BR ON 1:00
	10 X 50 F/S ON :50
	HOLD GOOD TECHNIQUE THROUGHOUT
SWIM:	DOWN EZ 200 STROKE

45. Mastering

SWIM:	500 YDS WARM-UP F/S
	2 X (KICK 50/SWIM 50) FOR 400 IM
PULL:	4 X 175 F/S ON 2:45
SWIM:	10 X 50 FLY ON 1:00
	10 X 50 BK ON 1:00
	10 X 50 BR ON 1:00
	10 X 50 F/S ON :50
	HOLD GOOD TECHNIQUE THROUGHOUT
SWIM:	DOWN EZ 200 STROKE

You only go around once, but if you work it right, once is enough.

130. Mastering

SWIM:	500 YDS F/S WARM UP
SWIM:	8 X 50 F/S ON :45
KICK:	16 X 25 IM ORDER ON :30
DRILL:	4 X 50 FLY ON 1:00
PULL:	2 X 400 F/S ON 6:00 *BREATHE 5*
SWIM:	(150 FLY + 50 BK + 100 BR + 100 F/S) ON 6:30
	(100 FLY + 100 BK + 150 BR + 100 F/S) ON 6:45
	(100 FLY + 150 BK + 50 BR + 100 F/S) ON 6:30
	(50 FLY + 100 BK + 100 BR + 150 F/S) ON 6:30
SWIM:	3 X (4 X 50 F/S) ON :40, :45, :55
SWIM:	DOWN EZ 200 CHOICE

46.Mastering

SWIM:	500 YDS WARM-UP ALL STROKES
KICK:	200 BK ON 4:00 +
	2 X 100 BR ON 2:00+
	4 X 50 F/S ON 1:00
PULL:	2 X 300 F/S
	WITH 10 SEC REST - BUILD EACH SWIM
SWIM:	6 X 25 FLY ON :30
	6 X (25 FLY + 25 BK) ON :55
	6 X (25 FLY + 25 BK + 25 BR) ON 1:20
	6 X 100 IM ON 1:45
KICK:	8 X 25 FLY ON :30
DRILL:	100 BK + 100 BR
SWIM:	8 X 50 F/S ALTERNATE ON:40 AND 45
SWIM:	DOWN EZ 200 F/S

46.Mastering

SWIM:	500 YDS WARM-UP ALL STROKES
KICK:	200 BK ON 4:00 +
	2 X 100 BR ON 2:00+
	4 X 50 F/S ON 1:00
PULL:	2 X 300 F/S
	WITH 10 SEC REST - BUILD EACH SWIM
SWIM:	6 X 25 FLY ON :30
	6 X (25 FLY + 25 BK) ON :55
	6 X (25 FLY + 25 BK + 25 BR) ON 1:20
	6 X 100 IM ON 1:45
KICK:	8 X 25 FLY ON :30
DRILL:	100 BK + 100 BR
SWIM:	8 X 50 F/S ALTERNATE ON:40 AND 45
SWIM:	DOWN EZ 200 F/S

I told my swimmers to go underwater and listen. They did. They came up, and said, "I don't hear anything." I replied, "I know; it's been like that all day!"

131. Mastering

SWIM:	500 YDS USE STROKES AND DRILLS
SWIM:	6 X 50 F/S ON :40
	6 X 50 BK ON :55
KICK:	12 X 50 IM ORDER ON 1:00
DRILL:	200 IM
SWIM:	10 X 50 ALTERNATE STROKE & F/S ON 1:00
SWIM:	6 X 50 BR ON 1:00
PULL:	3 X 200 F/S ON 3:00 *BREATHE 5*
SWIM:	2 X 200 STROKE FAST ON 4:00
SWIM:	DOWN EZ 200 F/S

47. Mastering

SWIM:	500 YDS F/S EZ
KICK:	6 X 50 BK ON 1:00
KICK:	6 X 100 CHOICE ON 2:00
PULL:	4 X (25 BR + 200 F/S) ON 3:30
SWIM:	18 X 50 ON 1:00 ALTERNATE FLY BR, F/S
SWIM:	200 BK OR BR ON 3:40
KICK:	200 WEAK STROKE
SPRINT:	4 X 25 BEST STROKE (NOT F/S) ON :45
SWIM:	DOWN EZ 200

47. Mastering

SWIM: 500 YDS F/S EZ
KICK: 6 X 50 BK ON 1:00
KICK: 6 X 100 CHOICE ON 2:00
PULL: 4 X (25 BR + 200 F/S) ON 3:30
SWIM: 18 X 50 ON 1:00 ALTERNATE FLY BR, F/S
SWIM: 200 BK OR BR ON 3:40
KICK: 200 WEAK STROKE
SPRINT: 4 X 25 BEST STROKE (NOT F/S) ON :45
SWIM: DOWN EZ 200

Desire makes winners in every walk of life.

132. Mastering

SWIM:	6 X (100 SWIM, 100 KICK, 100 PULL) ALL 4 STROKES + 2 CHOICE
SWIM:	6 X 150 BK ON 2:45
SWIM:	12 X 75 BR ON 1:30
SWIM:	6 X 100 F/S ON 1:30
SWIM:	12 X 25 ALTERNATE FLY & STROKE ON :45 FAST!
SWIM:	DOWN EZ 300 F/S

48. Mastering

SWIM:	500 YDS EZ WARM-UP F/S
SWIM:	16 X 25 ON :25 IM ORDER
KICK:	150 OF EACH STROKE IM ORDER ON 3:00
PULL:	8 X (25 STROKE + 100 F/S) ON 2:00
SWIM:	50 FLY + 200 IM ON 4 :15
	50 BK + 200 IM
	50 BR + 200 IM
	50 F/S + 200 IM
SWIM:	200 "A" STROKE (NOT F/S) ON 3:30
	200 "B" STROKE (NOT F/S) ON 3:30
SWIM:	DOWN EZ 200 F/S

48. Mastering

SWIM:	500 YDS EZ WARM-UP F/S
SWIM:	16 X 25 ON :25 IM ORDER
KICK:	150 OF EACH STROKE IM ORDER ON 3:00
PULL:	8 X (25 STROKE + 100 F/S) ON 2:00
SWIM:	50 FLY + 200 IM ON 4 :15
	50 BK + 200 IM
	50 BR + 200 IM
	50 F/S + 200 IM
SWIM:	200 "A" STROKE (NOT F/S) ON 3:30
	200 "B" STROKE (NOT F/S) ON 3:30
SWIM:	DOWN EZ 200 F/S

Eat a live toad the first thing in the morning, and nothing worse will happen to you the rest of the day.

133. Mastering

SWIM:	500 YDS EZ F/S
KICK:	200 STROKE + 200 F/S
SWIM:	6 X (75 F/S + 50 BR + 25 BK) ON 2:30
SWIM:	4 X 50 F/S ON :50 DESCEND
PULL:	600 F/S *BREATHE 3,5,3,5,3,5,PER 100*
SWIM:	4 X (50 FLY + 100 BK + 100 BR + 50 F/S) ON 5:45
SPRINT:	18 X 25 ON :45 USE 3 STROKES
SWIM:	DOWN EZ 200 STROKE

49. Mastering

SWIM:	500 YDS EZ USE 2 STROKES
KICK:	6 X 100 CHOICE ON 2:00
DRILL:	200 IM
SWIM:	75 STROKE ON 1:30
	2 X (2 X 50 F/S ON 1:30,
	4 X 25 STROKE ON :30)
DRILL:	100 BK
SWIM:	2 X (2 X 150 F/S ON 2:00,
	2 X 75 ON 1:00,
	2 X 25 F/S ON :20)
PULL:	4 X (100 F/S + 50 BR) ON 2:30
SPRINT:	8 X 50 ALTERNATE F/S
	AND CHOICE ON 1:00 (FAST)
SWIM:	DOWN EZ 200 STROKE

49. Mastering

SWIM:	500 YDS EZ USE 2 STROKES
KICK:	6 X 100 CHOICE ON 2:00
DRILL:	200 IM
SWIM:	75 STROKE ON 1:30
	2 X (2 X 50 F/S ON 1:30,
	4 X 25 STROKE ON :30)
DRILL:	100 BK
SWIM:	2 X (2 X 150 F/S ON 2:00,
	2 X 75 ON 1:00,
	2 X 25 F/S ON :20)
PULL:	4 X (100 F/S + 50 BR) ON 2:30
SPRINT:	8 X 50 ALTERNATE F/S
	AND CHOICE ON 1:00 (FAST)
SWIM:	DOWN EZ 200 STROKE

Attitudes are nothing more than habits of thought . . . and habits can be acquired.
Pacific Institute of America

134. Mastering

SWIM:	600 YDS USE F/S AND 2 STROKES
SWIM:	8 X (25 FLY + 50 F/S) ON 1:20 FAST
KICK:	6 X 50 ON 1:00 BR & FLY
KICK:	4 X 100 ON 2:00 BK & F/S
SWIM:	6 X (25 FLY + 50 STROKE) ON 1:45 FAST
PULL:	4 X (50 STROKE + 100 F/S) ON 2:45
SWIM:	4 X (25 FLY + 25 F/S) ON 1:00 FAST
SPRINT:	6 X 50 CHOICE NO F/S ON 1:15 DESCEND 1-3, 4-6
SWIM:	DOWN EZ 200 F/S

50. Mastering

SWIM:	500 YDS F/S AND 1 STROKE
SWIM:	4 X 50 F/S ON :40
	4 X 50 F/S ON :45
KICK:	16 X 50 IM ORDER ON 1:00
SWIM:	8 X (25 FLY + 100 BK OR BR) ON 2:15
SWIM:	6 X 100 BK OR BR ON 2:00
SWIM:	3 X 200 BK OR BR ON 3:50
SWIM:	3 X 150 F/S ON 2:10 HOLD 2:00
SWIM:	DOWN EZ 200 F/S

50. Mastering

SWIM:	500 YDS F/S AND 1 STROKE
SWIM:	4 X 50 F/S ON :40
	4 X 50 F/S ON :45
KICK:	16 X 50 IM ORDER ON 1:00
SWIM:	8 X (25 FLY + 100 BK OR BR) ON 2:15
SWIM:	6 X 100 BK OR BR ON 2:00
SWIM:	3 X 200 BK OR BR ON 3:50
SWIM:	3 X 150 F/S ON 2:10 HOLD 2:00
SWIM:	DOWN EZ 200 F/S

Attitudes are nothing more than habits of thought . . . and habits can be acquired.

Pacific Institute of America

135. Mastering

SWIM:	500 YDS F/S AND 1 STROKE
SPRINT:	5 X 75 F/S ON 1:00 3 X 75 F/S ON 1:10
KICK:	600 REVERSE IM ON 12:00
DRILL:	4 X 25 FLY ON :30
SWIM:	11 X 150 F/S WITH 5 SEC REST (1650 PACE)
SWIM:	200 EZ WITH DRILLS
SWIM:	8 X 30 YDS - i.e. 25 YDS + FAST TURNS ON 1:15 NO F/S
SWIM:	DOWN EZ 200 F/S

51. Mastering

SWIM:	500 YDS EZ USE ALL STROKES
SWIM:	8 X 75 F/S ON 1:00 HOLD :57
KICK:	500 AS 400 IM + 100 IM ON 10:15
PULL:	6 X 125 F/S ON 1:45
SWIM:	3 X 300 IM ON 5:00
	2 X 200 IM ON 3:15
	1 X 100 IM ON 1:30
DRILL:	100 BK
SWIM:	400 F/S ON 5:30 (BUILD)
	4 X 75 F/S ON 1:00 (PACE :55)
SWIM:	DOWN EZ 200 CHOICE

51. Mastering

SWIM:	500 YDS EZ USE ALL STROKES
SWIM:	8 X 75 F/S ON 1:00 HOLD :57
KICK:	500 AS 400 IM + 100 IM ON 10:15
PULL:	6 X 125 F/S ON 1:45
SWIM:	3 X 300 IM ON 5:00
	2 X 200 IM ON 3:15
	1 X 100 IM ON 1:30
DRILL:	100 BK
SWIM:	400 F/S ON 5:30 (BUILD)
	4 X 75 F/S ON 1:00 (PACE :55)
SWIM:	DOWN EZ 200 CHOICE

The power of hope upon human exertion and happiness is wonderful. Abraham Lincoln

136. Mastering

SWIM:	500 YDS CHOICE WARM UP
SWIM:	4 X 150 F/S ON 2:05 HOLD 2:00
KICK:	8 X 75 ALTERNATE ON 1:30
DRILL:	100 BK
PULL:	1,000 YDS NEGATIVE SPLIT EACH 200
SWIM:	400 STROKE CHECK 300 SPLIT *REST 30 SEC*
SWIM:	300 STROKE FASTER THAN PREVIOUS 300 CHECK 200 SPLIT *REST 30 SEC*
SWIM:	200 STROKE FASTER THAN PREVIOUS 200 CHECK 100 SPLIT.*REST 30 SEC*
SWIM:	100 STROKE FASTER THAN PREVIOUS 100 CHECK 50 SPLIT *REST 30 SEC*
SWIM:	50 STROKE FAST!!
SWIM:	DOWN EZ 200 F/S

52. Mastering

SWIM:	500 F/S EZ WARM-UP
SWIM:	20 X 25 F/S ON :25
KICK:	8 X 75 CHOICE ON 1:30
PULL:	2 X 400 F/S ON 6:00
	BREATHE 3,5,7, 9 PER 100
SWIM:	4 X (100 FLY + 25 BK + 25 BR ON 2:45)
	(100 BK + 25 BR + 25 F/S ON 2:45)
	(100 BR + 25 F/S ON 2 :15)
	REST 1 MIN
SPRINT:	8 X 25 F/S ON :40 (HOLD :16)
SWIM:	DOWN EZ 200 CHOICE

52. Mastering

SWIM:	500 F/S EZ WARM-UP
SWIM:	20 X 25 F/S ON :25
KICK:	8 X 75 CHOICE ON 1:30
PULL:	2 X 400 F/S ON 6:00
	BREATHE 3,5,7, 9 PER 100
SWIM:	4 X (100 FLY + 25 BK + 25 BR ON 2:45)
	(100 BK + 25 BR + 25 F/S ON 2:45)
	(100 BR + 25 F/S ON 2 :15)
	REST 1 MIN
SPRINT:	8 X 25 F/S ON :40 (HOLD :16)
SWIM:	DOWN EZ 200 CHOICE

One can never consent to creep when one feels an impulse to soar.
Helen Keller

137. Mastering

SWIM:	500 YDS USE ALL 4 STROKES
KICK:	6 X 100 CHOICE ON 2:00
SWIM:	10 X 50 STROKE ON 1:00
PULL:	2 X 300 F/S ON 4:30
	BREATHE 2,3,4 PER 100
SWIM:	3 X 200 STROKE OR IM
	ON 4:00
	DESCEND TIME
SWIM:	4 X (100 BK + 50 BR) ON 2:45
SWIM:	12 X 25 ALTERNATE F/S
	AND CHOICE ON :45 VERY FAST!
SWIM:	DOWN EZ 200 CHOICE

53. Mastering

SWIM: 500 YDS F/S AND 1 STROKE
KICK: 125 EACH STROKE IM ORDER ON 2:30
PULL: 8 X (75 F/S + 25 STROKE) ON 1:45
SWIM: 10 X 50 F/S, 5 ON :40, 5 ON :45
10 X 50 F/S, 5 ON :45, 5 ON :50
10 X 50 F/S, 5 ON :50, 5 ON :55
10 X 50 F/S, 5 ON :55, 5 ON 1:00
REDUCE TIMES AS REST INCREASES !
SPRINT: 4 X (4 X 25) IM ORDER ON :45
SWIM: DOWN EZ 200 STROKE

53. Mastering

SWIM: 500 YDS F/S AND 1 STROKE
KICK: 125 EACH STROKE IM ORDER ON 2:30
PULL: 8 X (75 F/S + 25 STROKE) ON 1:45
SWIM: 10 X 50 F/S, 5 ON :40, 5 ON :45
10 X 50 F/S, 5 ON :45, 5 ON :50
10 X 50 F/S, 5 ON :50, 5 ON :55
10 X 50 F/S, 5 ON :55, 5 ON 1:00
REDUCE TIMES AS REST INCREASES !
SPRINT: 4 X (4 X 25) IM ORDER ON :45
SWIM: DOWN EZ 200 STROKE

If it is worth doing at all, it is worth doing well.

138. Mastering

SWIM:	600 F/S WARM UP
KICK:	8 X (25 FLY + 25 BR + 25 F/S) ON 1:30
SWIM:	4 X 175 STROKE ON 3:30
	DESCEND TIMES
PULL:	2 X (100 CHOICE + 200 F/S) ON 5:00
SWIM:	16 X 50 IM ORDER ON 1:15
	GOOD QUALITY
DRILL:	SWIM 400 IM
SWIM:	8 X 25 CHOICE
	FAST BETWEEN FLAGS
SWIM:	DOWN EZ 200 F/S

54. Mastering

SWIM: 500 YDS EZ F/S
SWIM: 4 X (50 F/S ON :45 + 25 F/S ON :25)
KICK: 6 X 100 IM REVERSE ORDER ON 2:00
PULL: 2 X 400 F/S ON 6:00
BREATHE 5,7 PER 100
SWIM: 2 X(100 FLY + 50 BK + 50 BR+ 50 F/S ON 4 :15)
(50 FLY + 100 BK + 50 BR + 50 F/S ON 4 :15)
(50 FLY + 50 BK + 100 BR + 50 F/S ON 4 :15)
(50 FLY + 50 BK + 50 BR + 100 F/S ON 4 :15)
REST 1 MINUTE BETWEEN SETS
SPRINT: 4 X 25 F/S ON :45 *NO BREATHE*
SWIM: DOWN 200 EZ F/S

54. Mastering

SWIM: 500 YDS EZ F/S
SWIM: 4 X (50 F/S ON :45 + 25 F/S ON :25)
KICK: 6 X 100 IM REVERSE ORDER ON 2:00
PULL: 2 X 400 F/S ON 6:00
BREATHE 5,7 PER 100
SWIM: 2 X(100 FLY + 50 BK + 50 BR+ 50 F/S ON 4 :15)
(50 FLY + 100 BK + 50 BR + 50 F/S ON 4 :15)
(50 FLY + 50 BK + 100 BR + 50 F/S ON 4 :15)
(50 FLY + 50 BK + 50 BR + 100 F/S ON 4 :15)
REST 1 MINUTE BETWEEN SETS
SPRINT: 4 X 25 F/S ON :45 *NO BREATHE*
SWIM: DOWN 200 EZ F/S

Doing a thing nearly right and doing it exactly right is usually the difference between success and failure.

139. Mastering

SWIM:	500 CHOICE WARM UP
PULL:	700 *BREATHE EVERY 5TH STROKE*
SWIM:	10 X 50 F/S ON :40 PACE :36
KICK:	8 X 100 ALTERNATE F/S AND CHOICE ON 2:00
SWIM:	8 X 75 ON 1:30 ALTERNATE EZ F/S & FAST STROKE
SWIM:	8 X (25 EZ F/S + 50 FAST STROKE) ON 2:00
SPRINT:	12 X 25 ALTERNATE F/S AND STROKE ON 1:00
SWIM:	DOWN EZ 200 F/S

55. Mastering

SWIM:	500 YDS EZ CHOICE
SWIM:	12 X 25 IM ORDER ON :25
KICK:	600 CHOICE (25 EZ, 25 HARD)
DRILL:	100 BK
PULL:	4 X (25 BR + 100 F/S) ON 2:00
SWIM:	3 X (200 BK OR BR) ON 2:45
	2 X (100 FLY + 100 BK) ON 3:45
	2 X (100 BR + 100 F/S) ON 3:45
	2 X 200 IM ON 3:45
	REST 1 MINUTE
SPRINT:	4 X 25 FLY, *BREATHE 3 ON :45*
SWIM:	DOWN EZ 200

55. Mastering

SWIM:	500 YDS EZ CHOICE
SWIM:	12 X 25 IM ORDER ON :25
KICK:	600 CHOICE (25 EZ, 25 HARD)
DRILL:	100 BK
PULL:	4 X (25 BR + 100 F/S) ON 2:00
SWIM:	3 X (200 BK OR BR) ON 2:45
	2 X (100 FLY + 100 BK) ON 3:45
	2 X (100 BR + 100 F/S) ON 3:45
	2 X 200 IM ON 3:45
	REST 1 MINUTE
SPRINT:	4 X 25 FLY, *BREATHE 3 ON :45*
SWIM:	DOWN EZ 200

Doing a thing nearly right and doing it exactly right is usually the difference between success and failure.

140. Mastering

SWIM:	500 YDS F/S EZ
KICK:	14 X 50 CHOICE ON 1:00
SWIM:	8 X 75 F/S ON 1:00 HOLD :56
PULL:	2 X (400 F/S + 100 STROKE) ON 7:30
SWIM:	4 X (200 F/S FAST + 100 IM EZ) ON 5:30
SWIM:	8 X (25 YDS + TURN) F/S ON 1:15
SWIM:	DOWN EZ 200 STROKE

56. Mastering

SWIM:	500 YDS F/S EZ WARM-UP
SWIM:	8 X 200 F/S ON 2:50
	1 X 50 ON :40
KICK:	400 IM REVERSE ORDER
DRILL:	100 IM
SWIM:	6 X (25 FLY + 50 BK) ON 1:20
	6 X (25 BK + 50 BR) ON 1:20
	6 X (25 BR + 50 F/S) ON 1:15
SWIM:	DOWN EZ 200

56. Mastering

SWIM:	500 YDS F/S EZ WARM-UP
SWIM:	8 X 200 F/S ON 2:50
	1 X 50 ON :40
KICK:	400 IM REVERSE ORDER
DRILL:	100 IM
SWIM:	6 X (25 FLY + 50 BK) ON 1:20
	6 X (25 BK + 50 BR) ON 1:20
	6 X (25 BR + 50 F/S) ON 1:15
SWIM:	DOWN EZ 200

The highest reward for man's toil is not what he 'gets for it,' but what he 'becomes by it.' *Ruskin*

141. Mastering

SWIM:	500 YDS CHOICE EZ
SWIM:	8 X 75 F/S ON 1:15 HOLD:55
KICK:	6 X 100 CHOICE ON 2:00
PULL:	4 X 125 STROKE ON 3:00
SWIM:	8 X (25 FLY + 75 STROKE) ON 2:30
SWIM:	8 X (25 BK + 50 STROKE + 25 F/S) ON 2:30
SPRINT:	8 X 50 F/S ON 1:15
SWIM:	DOWN EZ 200 F/S

57. Mastering

SWIM: 500 YDS EZ WARM-UP
6 X (KICK 100/SWIM 50)
ONE EACH STROKE IM ORDER +
2 CHOICE ON 3:00

DRILL: 100 IM

SWIM: 4 X (25 F/S ON :25
100 IM ON 1:45
400 F/S ON 5:45
100 STROKE ON 1:45)
REST 1 MINUTE BETWEEN SETS

SPRINT: 4 X (25 STROKE + 25 F/S) ON 1:00

SWIM: DOWN EZ 200 STROKE

57. Mastering

SWIM: 500 YDS EZ WARM-UP
6 X (KICK 100/SWIM 50)
ONE EACH STROKE IM ORDER +
2 CHOICE ON 3:00

DRILL: 100 IM

SWIM: 4 X (25 F/S ON :25
100 IM ON 1:45
400 F/S ON 5:45
100 STROKE ON 1:45)
REST 1 MINUTE BETWEEN SETS

SPRINT: 4 X (25 STROKE + 25 F/S) ON 1:00

SWIM: DOWN EZ 200 STROKE

Endurance is the result of a decision made from within.

142. Mastering

SWIM: 500 YDS CHOICE WARM UP

SWIM: 6 X 100 IM ON 2:00 HOLD 1:26

KICK: 8 X 75
ALTERNATE F/S AND STROKE
ON 1:30

PULL: 600 F/S WITH EACH 4TH 25 BREAST

SWIM: 200 STROKE + 200 F/S
GOOD TECHNIQUE
TEAM PRACTICE RELAYS
OFF BLOCKS
4 X 50 FLY *GOOD STARTS!*
2 X 50 BR *GOOD TAKE OFFS!*
2 X 50 BK *GOOD TURNS!*
6 X 50 F/S *GOOD FINISHES!*
GOOD FUN!!

SWIM: DOWN EZ 200 F/S

58. Mastering

SWIM:	500 YDS F/S EZ WARM-UP
SWIM:	10 X 50 F/S ON :45
KICK:	200 OF EACH STROKE IM ORDER + 100 IM CONTINUOUS
PULL:	4 X (25 FLY + 100 BK) ON 2 :15
	4 X (25 BK + 100 BR) ON 2:30
	4 X (25 BR + 100 F/S) ON 2:00
	4 X (100 IM + 25 F/S) ON 2 :15
DRILL:	100 CHOICE
SPRINT:	4 X 25 FLY ON :45 *BREATHE 3,2,1*
SWIM:	DOWN EZ 200 F/S

58. Mastering

SWIM:	500 YDS F/S EZ WARM-UP
SWIM:	10 X 50 F/S ON :45
KICK:	200 OF EACH STROKE IM ORDER + 100 IM CONTINUOUS
PULL:	4 X (25 FLY + 100 BK) ON 2 :15
	4 X (25 BK + 100 BR) ON 2:30
	4 X (25 BR + 100 F/S) ON 2:00
	4 X (100 IM + 25 F/S) ON 2 :15
DRILL:	100 CHOICE
SPRINT:	4 X 25 FLY ON :45 *BREATHE 3,2,1*
SWIM:	DOWN EZ 200 F/S

Endurance is the result of a decision made from within.

143. Mastering

SWIM:	600 YDS ALL 4 STROKES WARM UP
KICK:	300 IM STRAIGHT AND REVERSE
PULL:	2 X 400 F/S ON 6:00
	BREATHE EVERY 5
SWIM:	4 X 100 IM ON 2:00 DESCEND
DRILL:	4 X 50 FLY ON 1:00
SWIM:	8 X 75 F/S ON 1:05 HOLD :55
SPRINT:	10 X (25 + TURN) ON 1:15
SWIM:	DOWN EZ 200 F/S

59. Mastering

SWIM:	500 YDS ALL 4 STROKES
SWIM:	8 X 75 F/S ON 1:10 HOLD :56
KICK:	6 X 100 CHOICE ON 2:00
PULL:	8 X (50 STROKE + 50 F/S) ON 2:00
SWIM:	8 X (25 FLY + 50 STROKE + 25 F/S) ON 1:45
SWIM:	4 X 150 F/S ON 2 :10 HOLD 2:00
SPRINT:	8 X 25 STROKE ON :45(95%SPEED)
SWIM:	DOWN EZ 200 CHOICE

59. Mastering

SWIM:	500 YDS ALL 4 STROKES
SWIM:	8 X 75 F/S ON 1:10 HOLD :56
KICK:	6 X 100 CHOICE ON 2:00
PULL:	8 X (50 STROKE + 50 F/S) ON 2:00
SWIM:	8 X (25 FLY + 50 STROKE + 25 F/S) ON 1:45
SWIM:	4 X 150 F/S ON 2 :10 HOLD 2:00
SPRINT:	8 X 25 STROKE ON :45(95%SPEED)
SWIM:	DOWN EZ 200 CHOICE

The race is not always to the swift, but to those who keep on swimming.

144. Mastering

SWIM:	500 YDS EZ WARM UP
SWIM:	4 X 150 F/S ON 2:10 HOLD 2:00
KICK:	20 X 25 ALTERNATE STROKE AND F/S ON :30
PULL:	800 F/S AS (75 EZ + 25 FAST)
SWIM:	8 X (50 STROKE FAST ON 1:30 + 100 EZ F/S) ON EVERY 4:00
SWIM:	DOWN EZ 200 STROKE

60. Mastering

SWIM:	500 YDS F/S WARM-UP
SWIM:	4 X 50 FLY ON 1:00
SWIM:	8 X 50 F/S ON :45
KICK:	500 AS EZ 25, HARD 25, (CHOICE)
DRILL:	8 X 25 F/S ON :30
PULL:	3 X 300 F/S ON 4:20
	BREATHE 3, 5, 7 PER 100
SWIM:	4 X(100 IM ON 1:45 + 200 STROKE ON 4:00)
SWIM:	16 X 25 ON :30 HOLD :16
SWIM:	DOWN EZ 200 F/S

60. Mastering

SWIM:	500 YDS F/S WARM-UP
SWIM:	4 X 50 FLY ON 1:00
SWIM:	8 X 50 F/S ON :45
KICK:	500 AS EZ 25, HARD 25, (CHOICE)
DRILL:	8 X 25 F/S ON :30
PULL:	3 X 300 F/S ON 4:20
	BREATHE 3, 5, 7 PER 100
SWIM:	4 X(100 IM ON 1:45 + 200 STROKE ON 4:00)
SWIM:	16 X 25 ON :30 HOLD :16
SWIM:	DOWN EZ 200 F/S

The race is not always to the swift, but to those who keep on swimming.

145. Mastering

SWIM:	800 YDS USING STROKES AND DRILLS WARM UP
KICK:	12 X 50 CHOICE ON 1:05
DRILL:	200 REVERSE IM
SWIM:	200 IM (90% EFFORT)
SWIM:	500 F/S *ACCENTUATE TECHNIQUE*, MODERATE PACE
DRILL:	100 BK
SPRINT:	4 X 25 FLY ON :40 *REST 30 SEC*
	4 X 50 BK ON 1:15 *REST 30 SEC*
	4 X 75 BR ON 2:00 *REST 30 SEC*
	4 X 100 F/S ON 3:00
SWIM:	DOWN EZ 200 F/S

61. Mastering

SWIM: 500 YDS EZ CHOICE
(DRILL 25 F/S + SWIM 100 F/S) X 5
ON 2:00
KICK: 20 X 25 ON :30 CHOICE OF STROKES
PULL: 400 F/S, *BREATHE 3, 5, 5, 7 PER 100*
SWIM: 3 X(50 FLY + 25 BK + 25 BR + 25 F/S
ON 2 :10)
(25 FLY + 50 BK + 25 BR + 25 F/S
ON 2 :10)
(25 FLY + 25 BK + 50 BR + 25 F/S
ON 2 :10)
(25 FLY + 25 BK + 25 BR + 50 F/S
ON 2 :10)
SWIM: 100 EZ CHOICE
SWIM: 3 X 100 IM ON 2:00 DESCEND
SWIM: 200 EZ DOWN CHOICE

61. Mastering

SWIM: 500 YDS EZ CHOICE
(DRILL 25 F/S + SWIM 100 F/S) X 5
ON 2:00
KICK: 20 X 25 ON :30 CHOICE OF STROKES
PULL: 400 F/S, *BREATHE 3, 5, 5, 7 PER 100*
SWIM: 3 X(50 FLY + 25 BK + 25 BR + 25 F/S
ON 2 :10)
(25 FLY + 50 BK + 25 BR + 25 F/S
ON 2 :10)
(25 FLY + 25 BK + 50 BR + 25 F/S
ON 2 :10)
(25 FLY + 25 BK + 25 BR + 50 F/S
ON 2 :10)
SWIM: 100 EZ CHOICE
SWIM: 3 X 100 IM ON 2:00 DESCEND
SWIM: 200 EZ DOWN CHOICE

The time is always right to do what is right.
Martin Luther King, Jr.

146. Mastering

SWIM:	500 YDS EZ F/S
KICK:	16 X 50
	ALTERNATE F/S AND CHOICE
	ON 1:05
PULL:	2 X 400 F/S ON 5:45
SWIM:	1 X 400 BEST STROKE ON 7:00
DRILL:	200 IM
SWIM:	1 X 400 2ND BEST STROKE ON 7:20
SWIM:	100 F/S EZ
SWIM:	32 X 25 IM ORDER ON :30
SWIM:	DOWN EZ 200 STROKE

62. Mastering

SWIM:	500 YDS WARM UP F/S
KICK:	20 X 25 IM ORDER ON :30
DRILL:	4 X 50 ON 1:10
PULL:	3 X (150 F/S + 50 STROKE) ON 3 :15
SWIM:	5 X 200 F/S ON 2:45 HOLD 2:40
SWIM:	4 X (50 FLY + 50 BK) ON 1:45
SWIM:	(50 STROKE + 50 BR + 50 F/S) X 4 ON 2:30
SWIM:	200 IM REVERSE ORDER FOR TIME
SPRINT:	4 X 50 F / 5 ON :50 HOLD :36
SWIM:	DOWN EZ 200 F/S

62. Mastering

SWIM:	500 YDS WARM UP F/S
KICK:	20 X 25 IM ORDER ON :30
DRILL:	4 X 50 ON 1:10
PULL:	3 X (150 F/S + 50 STROKE) ON 3 :15
SWIM:	5 X 200 F/S ON 2:45 HOLD 2:40
SWIM:	4 X (50 FLY + 50 BK) ON 1:45
SWIM:	(50 STROKE + 50 BR + 50 F/S) X 4 ON 2:30
SWIM:	200 IM REVERSE ORDER FOR TIME
SPRINT:	4 X 50 F / 5 ON :50 HOLD :36
SWIM:	DOWN EZ 200 F/S

The time is always right to do what is right.
Martin Luther King, Jr.

147. Mastering

SWIM:	500 YDS F/S AND 1 STROKE WARM UP
SWIM:	6 X (25 F/S ON :20 + 50 F/S ON :45)
KICK:	16 X 25 BUILD CHOICE ON :30
PULL:	5 X (25 FLY + 25 BR + 50 F/S) CONTINUOUSLY
SWIM:	10 X 50 F/S ON :45
	1 X 200 FLY EZ
	20 X 25 F/S ON :25
	1 X 200 BK EZ 500 F/S ON 6:40
	1 X 200 BR EZ
SWIM:	4 X 25 BEST STROKE ON :30 *NO BREATHE LAST 10 YDS.*
SWIM:	DOWN EZ 200 F/S

63. Mastering

SWIM: 500 YDS EZ F/S AND 1 STROKE
SWIM: 4 X 125 F/S ON 1:50
KICK: 500 CHOICE ON 10:00
DRILL: 4 X 50 IM ORDER ON 1:00
PULL: 8 X 75 F/5 ON 1 :10, *BREATHE 3 & 5* ALTERNATE 75
SWIM: 8 X (25 FLY + 50 STROKE + 75 F/S) ON 2:20
SWIM: 4 X (25 STROKE IM ORDER FAST + 100 F/S MODERATE) ON 2:15
SPRINT: 8 X 50 ALTERNATE STROKE AND F/S ON :55
SWIM: DOWN EZ 200 CHOICE

63. Mastering

SWIM: 500 YDS EZ F/S AND 1 STROKE
SWIM: 4 X 125 F/S ON 1:50
KICK: 500 CHOICE ON 10:00
DRILL: 4 X 50 IM ORDER ON 1:00
PULL: 8 X 75 F/5 ON 1 :10, *BREATHE 3 & 5* ALTERNATE 75
SWIM: 8 X (25 FLY + 50 STROKE + 75 F/S) ON 2:20
SWIM: 4 X (25 STROKE IM ORDER FAST + 100 F/S MODERATE) ON 2:15
SPRINT: 8 X 50 ALTERNATE STROKE AND F/S ON :55
SWIM: DOWN EZ 200 CHOICE

Every day, in every way, I am getting better and better and better.
Silva Mind Control

148. Mastering

SWIM:	500 YDS EZ WARM-UP
KICK:	10 X 50 CHOICE ON 1:00
PULL:	200 IM STRAIGHT AND REVERSED
SWIM:	10 X 50 F/S ON :45
	5 X 100 F/S ON 1:25
	2 X 250 F/S ON 3:35
	1 X 500 F/S ON 6:45
SPRINT:	20 X 25 ON :40 IM ORDER
SWIM:	DOWN EZ 200 STROKE

64. Mastering

SWIM:	500 YDS F/S EZ
SWIM:	8 X 50 F/S ON :45 HOLD :39
KICK:	100 FLY + 100 BK + 100 BR ON 6:00
KICK:	4 X 50 F/S ON 1:05
PULL:	4 X (50 FLY + 50 BK + 50 F/S) ON 3:00
SWIM:	4 X (25 BK + 100 BR) ON 2:15
SWIM:	500 F/S ON 7:00, *BREATHE 5*
SWIM:	4 X (100 STROKE + 25 F/S) ON 2:15
SWIM:	12 X 25 F/S ON :25 AND :20 ALTERNATELY
SWIM:	DOWN EZ 200 F/S

64. Mastering

SWIM:	500 YDS F/S EZ
SWIM:	8 X 50 F/S ON :45 HOLD :39
KICK:	100 FLY + 100 BK + 100 BR ON 6:00
KICK:	4 X 50 F/S ON 1:05
PULL:	4 X (50 FLY + 50 BK + 50 F/S) ON 3:00
SWIM:	4 X (25 BK + 100 BR) ON 2:15
SWIM:	500 F/S ON 7:00, *BREATHE 5*
SWIM:	4 X (100 STROKE + 25 F/S) ON 2:15
SWIM:	12 X 25 F/S ON :25 AND :20 ALTERNATELY
SWIM:	DOWN EZ 200 F/S

Support water sports. Date a swimmer!

149. Mastering

SWIM:	500 CHOICE EZ WARM UP
KICK:	400 IM
PULL:	100 YDS - 200 YDS - 300 YDS F/S
	ON - 1:45 - 3:00 - 4:30
SWIM:	4 X (100 IM + 25 FLY) ON 2:30
	4 X (100 IM + 25 BK) ON 2:30
	4 X (100 IM + 25 BR) ON 2:30
	4 X (100 IM + 25 F/S) ON 2:30
	HOLD 2:00
DRILL:	200 FLY
SPRINT:	4 SETS OF 5 X 25 F/S AS
	1ST ON :20
	2ND ON :25
	3RD ON :30
	4TH ON :40
SWIM:	DOWN EZ 200 F/S

65. Mastering

SWIM: 500 YDS EZ CHOICE
4 X (200 F/S + KICK 200 CHOICE
+PULL 200 F/S) ON 10:00
SWIM: 8 X 100 F/S ON 1:30 HOLD 1:16
DRILL: 200 STROKE
SWIM: 8 X 50 ON 1:00
ALTERNATE F/S AND FLY
SWIM: DOWN EZ 200 CHOICE

65. Mastering

SWIM: 500 YDS EZ CHOICE
4 X (200 F/S + KICK 200 CHOICE
+PULL 200 F/S) ON 10:00
SWIM: 8 X 100 F/S ON 1:30 HOLD 1:16
DRILL: 200 STROKE
SWIM: 8 X 50 ON 1:00
ALTERNATE F/S AND FLY
SWIM: DOWN EZ 200 CHOICE

Nobody can make you feel inferior without your consent.

150. Mastering

SWIM:	500 YDS F/S WARM UP
SWIM:	8 X 75 F/S ON 1:05 HOLD :56
KICK:	5 X 100 IM ON 2:00
DRILL:	2 X 50 BK ON 1:00
PULL:	6 X (50 STROKE + 50 F/S) ON 1:50
SWIM:	11 X (25 F/S ON :20 + 100 F/S ON 1:30 + 25 F/S ON :25)
	NO REST UNLESS EARNED
SWIM:	DOWN EZ 200 CHOICE

66. Mastering

SWIM:	500 YDS EZ F/S AND 2 OTHER STROKES
SWIM:	16 X 25 IM ORDER ON :30
KICK:	8 X (50 F/S + 25 STROKE) ON 1:30
PULL:	300 F/S - 200 F/S - 100 F/S ON 4:30 - 3:00- 1:25
SWIM:	6 X 300 IM ON 5:00 DESCEND IN GROUPS OF 2, i.e. 1&2, 3&4, 5&6
SPRINT:	4 X (3 X 25 F/S + 1 X 25 FLY) ON :25
SWIM:	DOWN EZ 200 STROKE

66. Mastering

SWIM:	500 YDS EZ F/S AND 2 OTHER STROKES
SWIM:	16 X 25 IM ORDER ON :30
KICK:	8 X (50 F/S + 25 STROKE) ON 1:30
PULL:	300 F/S - 200 F/S - 100 F/S ON 4:30 - 3:00- 1:25
SWIM:	6 X 300 IM ON 5:00 DESCEND IN GROUPS OF 2, i.e. 1&2, 3&4, 5&6
SPRINT:	4 X (3 X 25 F/S + 1 X 25 FLY) ON :25
SWIM:	DOWN EZ 200 STROKE

The key word to success in sports is confidence. *Mario Andretti*

151. Mastering

SWIM:	500 YDS CHOICE
SWIM:	4 X 150 F/S ON 2 :10 HOLD 1:55
KICK:	10 X 50 F/S BUILD ON 1:05
SWIM:	3 X (200 IM + 50 FLY) ON 4:15
	3 X (200 IM + 50 BK) ON 4 :15
	3 X (200 IM + 50 BR) ON 4:15
	3 X (200 IM + 50 F/S) ON 4 :15
	TRY TO HOLD 4:00
SWIM:	DOWN EZ 200 STROKE

67. Mastering

SWIM:	500 YDS CHOICE WARM UP
SWIM:	6 X 100 F/S ON 1:30 HOLD 1:15
KICK:	8 X 100 IM ON 2:05
PULL:	4 X 200 F/S LAST 25 STROKE ON 3:15
SWIM:	100 STROKE ON 1:45
	200 F/S ON 2:45
	300 STROKE ON 5:15
	400 F/S ON 5:45
	300 IM ON 5:15
	200 F/S ON 2:50
	100 IM ON 1:45
SWIM:	DOWN EZ 200 F/S

67. Mastering

SWIM: 500 YDS CHOICE WARM UP
SWIM: 6 X 100 F/S ON 1:30 HOLD 1:15
KICK: 8 X 100 IM ON 2:05
PULL: 4 X 200 F/S LAST 25 STROKE ON 3:15
SWIM: 100 STROKE ON 1:45
200 F/S ON 2:45
300 STROKE ON 5:15
400 F/S ON 5:45
300 IM ON 5:15
200 F/S ON 2:50
100 IM ON 1:45
SWIM: DOWN EZ 200 F/S

The key word to success in sports is confidence. *Mario Andretti*

152. Mastering

SWIM:	500 YDS EZ F/S
SWIM:	12 X 25 F/S ON :30
PULL:	4 X 125 ON 2:30 AS (100 F/S + 25 BR)
SWIM:	8 X 50 BR ON :55
	4 X 100 F/S ON 1:20
	4 X 100 F/S ON 1:25 HOLD 1:11
	4 X 100 F/S ON 1:30 HOLD 1:19
	4 X 100 F/S ON 2:00 HOLD 1:16
SWIM:	16 X 25 4 EACH STROKE IM ORDER, FLY & BR ON :40, BK & F/S ON :30
SWIM:	DOWN EZ 200 CHOICE

68. Mastering

SWIM:	500 YDS F/S EZ
SWIM:	8 X 75 STROKE ON 1:30
PULL:	4 X (125 F/S + 25 STROKE) ON 2:15
SWIM:	6 X 125 F/S ON 1:45
	6 X 75 F/S ON 1:05
	6 X 50 F/S ON :40
	6 X 25 F/S ON :25
	NO REST IN BETWEEN ABOVE SETS!
DRILL:	100 BK
SWIM:	4 X 50 STROKE ON :55
SWIM:	DOWN 200 EZ F/S

68. Mastering

SWIM:	500 YDS F/S EZ
SWIM:	8 X 75 STROKE ON 1:30
PULL:	4 X (125 F/S + 25 STROKE) ON 2:15
SWIM:	6 X 125 F/S ON 1:45
	6 X 75 F/S ON 1:05
	6 X 50 F/S ON :40
	6 X 25 F/S ON :25
	NO REST IN BETWEEN ABOVE SETS!
DRILL:	100 BK
SWIM:	4 X 50 STROKE ON :55
SWIM:	DOWN 200 EZ F/S

The swimmer who says, "It can't be done" is passed by the swimmer who is doing it.

153. Mastering

SWIM:	500 YDS F/S WARM UP
KICK:	16 X 25 IM ORDER ON :30 + 100 BR ON 2:00
SWIM:	8 X 75 F/S ON 1:30 HOLD :52
PULL:	500 F/S BREATHE 3, 5 ALTERNATE 100
SWIM:	100 FLY + 50 BK ON 3:00 100 BK + 50 BR ON 3:00 100 BR + 50 F/S ON 3:00 REPEAT 4 TIMES
SWIM:	8 X (25 F/S FAST ON :30 + 50 F/S EZ ON 1:30)
SWIM:	DOWN EZ 200 STROKE

69. Mastering

SWIM:	500 YDS F/S EZ WARM UP
KICK:	5 X 100 ALTERNATE F/S AND CHOICE ON 2:00
DRILL:	(50 FLY + SWIM 50 FLY) X 6 ON 2:10
PULL:	3 X (100 BK + 200 BR + 200 F/S) ON 7:00
SWIM:	8 X 150 IM OMIT ONE STROKE EACH IN IM ORDER ON 2:30
DRILL:	4 X 50 FLY ON 1:00
SWIM:	16 X 25 F/S, AS 6 ON :20, 6 ON :25, 4 ON :45 HOLD :18
SWIM:	DOWN 200 EZ STROKE

69. Mastering

SWIM:	500 YDS F/S EZ WARM UP
KICK:	5 X 100 ALTERNATE F/S AND CHOICE ON 2:00
DRILL:	(50 FLY + SWIM 50 FLY) X 6 ON 2:10
PULL:	3 X (100 BK + 200 BR + 200 F/S) ON 7:00
SWIM:	8 X 150 IM OMIT ONE STROKE EACH IN IM ORDER ON 2:30
DRILL:	4 X 50 FLY ON 1:00
SWIM:	16 X 25 F/S, AS 6 ON :20, 6 ON :25, 4 ON :45 HOLD :18
SWIM:	DOWN 200 EZ STROKE

A mobile section of petrified matter agglomerates no bryophytes.

154. Mastering

SWIM:	500 YDS CHOICE WARM UP
KICK:	8 X 100 IM ORDER ON 2:00
SWIM:	10 X 50 F/S ON 1:00 HOLD:34
	10 X 50 F/S ON 1:15 HOLD :32
PULL:	5 X (100 F/S + 25 STROKE) CONTINUOUS
SWIM:	2 X 400 F/S ON 5:45 HOLD 5:25
SWIM:	DOWN EZ 200 F/S

70. Mastering

SWIM: 500 YDS EZ USE ANY 2 STROKES
DRILL: 400 IM, 3 RIGHT ARM, 3 LEFT ARM AND 3 SWIM
SWIM: 8 X 50 F/S ON :40 HOLD :35
DRILL: (DRILL 100 + SWIM 100) EACH STROKE IM ORDER
PULL: 6 X (25 BR + 100 F/S + 25 BR) ON 2:30
SWIM: 6 X (200 F/S ON 3:00 + 50 FLY ON :50) ON 4:00
SPRINT: 4 X 50 BK ON 1:00
SWIM: DOWN EZ 200 F/S

70. Mastering

SWIM: 500 YDS EZ USE ANY 2 STROKES
DRILL: 400 IM, 3 RIGHT ARM, 3 LEFT ARM AND 3 SWIM
SWIM: 8 X 50 F/S ON :40 HOLD :35
DRILL: (DRILL 100 + SWIM 100) EACH STROKE IM ORDER
PULL: 6 X (25 BR + 100 F/S + 25 BR) ON 2:30
SWIM: 6 X (200 F/S ON 3:00 + 50 FLY ON :50) ON 4:00
SPRINT: 4 X 50 BK ON 1:00
SWIM: DOWN EZ 200 F/S

That you may fail is not a sufficient reason for not trying.

155. Mastering

SWIM:	500 YDS F/S EZ	
KICK:	300 IM STRAIGHT AND REVERSED	
SWIM:	4 X	(25 STROKE ON :30 + 50 F/S ON 1:00 HOLD :36 + 75 F/S ON 2:00 HOLD :54)
PULL:	2 X 400 F/S ON 6:00 BREATHE 5, 7 PER 200	
SWIM:	4 X (50 FLY + 50 BK + 100 BR ON 3:30) (50 BK + 50 BR + 100 F/S ON 3:30) (50 BR + 50 F/S + 100 FLY ON 3:30) *1 MINUTE REST BETWEEN SETS*	
SPRINT:	8 X 25 FLY ON :40 *BREATHE EVERY 3*	
SWIM:	DOWN EZ 200 STROKE	

71. Mastering

SWIM:	500 YDS F/S WARM UP
KICK:	5 X 100 IM ON 2:05
DRILL:	100 IM REVERSE ORDER
SWIM:	12 X 25 F/S ON :25 HOLD :17
PULL:	500 F/S, BREATHE 3,5,7,9,3 PER 100
SWIM:	5 X 100 F/S ON 1:20 HOLD 1:16
SWIM:	3 X 200 BK OR BR ON 3:30
SWIM:	8 X 25 FLY ON :45 HOLD :20
SWIM:	3 X 200 IM, #2 REVERSE ORDER ON 3:45
SWIM:	DOWN 200 EZ F/S

71. Mastering

SWIM:	500 YDS F/S WARM UP
KICK:	5 X 100 IM ON 2:05
DRILL:	100 IM REVERSE ORDER
SWIM:	12 X 25 F/S ON :25 HOLD :17
PULL:	500 F/S, BREATHE 3,5,7,9,3 PER 100
SWIM:	5 X 100 F/S ON 1:20 HOLD 1:16
SWIM:	3 X 200 BK OR BR ON 3:30
SWIM:	8 X 25 FLY ON :45 HOLD :20
SWIM:	3 X 200 IM, #2 REVERSE ORDER ON 3:45
SWIM:	DOWN 200 EZ F/S

Are you prepared to win if you get the chance?

156. Mastering

SWIM:	500 YDS ALL STROKES WARM UP
KICK:	200 CHOICE + 6 X 50 F/S ON 1:00
SWIM:	16 X 25 F/S BUILD ON :40
PULL:	4 X (50 BR + 50 BK + 100 F/S) ON 3:15
SWIM:	8 X (25 FLY + 100 F/S + 25 FLY) ON 2:30
SWIM:	3 X (12 X 25 F/S) 1ST SET - ON :20, 2ND ON :25, 3RD ON :45 *REST 2:00 BETWEEN SETS*
SWIM:	DOWN EZ 200 F/S

72. Mastering

SWIM: 500 YDS EZ WARM UP
PULL: 500 YDS BUILD FROM 1:35/ 100 F/S TO 1:25 *REST 30 SEC*
KICK: 5 X 100 ON 1:55 AND 2:00 ALTERNATELY
SWIM: 25 YDS + 5 SEC + 50 YDS + 5 SEC UP TO 325 YDS AND BACK DOWN TO 25 AGAIN

i.e. 1 LENGTH + 5 SEC, 2 LENGTHS + 5 SEC,..., 13 AND 12 LENGTHS, 11 LENGTHS,... FOR TOTAL OF 4,225 YDS

1 HOUR DISTANCE AT 1:24/100 F/S PACE.
SWIM: DOWN 200 EZ

72. Mastering

SWIM: 500 YDS EZ WARM UP
PULL: 500 YDS BUILD FROM 1:35/ 100 F/S TO 1:25 *REST 30 SEC*
KICK: 5 X 100 ON 1:55 AND 2:00 ALTERNATELY
SWIM: 25 YDS + 5 SEC + 50 YDS + 5 SEC UP TO 325 YDS AND BACK DOWN TO 25 AGAIN

i.e. 1 LENGTH + 5 SEC, 2 LENGTHS + 5 SEC,..., 13 AND 12 LENGTHS, 11 LENGTHS,... FOR TOTAL OF 4,225 YDS

1 HOUR DISTANCE AT 1:24/100 F/S PACE.
SWIM: DOWN 200 EZ

If living your own life seems difficult, remember that no one has ever attempted your life before. *Tom Jackson*

157. Mastering

SWIM:	500 F/S WARM UP EZ	
SWIM:	10 X 50 F/S ON :50 HOLD :35	
KICK:	10 X 50 AS (25 EZ + 25 FAST) F/S ON 1:00	
PULL:	500 F/S EVERY 4TH 25 BREAST	
SWIM:	2 X	(50 FLY + 50 BK ON 2:00
		(50 BK + 50 BR ON 2:00
		(50 BR + 50 F/S ON 2:00)
SWIM:	4 X 100 IM ON 1:45 DESCEND	
SWIM:	16 X 50 AS 8 F/S, 8 STROKE ON 1:00	
SWIM:	DOWN EZ 200 CHOICE	

73. Mastering

SWIM:	500 YDS EZ ALL 4 STROKES
SWIM:	12 X 25 ON :30 IM ORDER
SWIM:	8 X 25 F/S ON :25
KICK:	8 X 75 ALTERNATE F/S AND STROKE ON 1:30
DRILL:	200 BR (2 KICKS TO 1 PULL)
SWIM:	200 F/S BUILD FROM :45/:50 TO :40/:50 *REST 30 SEC*
SWIM:	4 X 200 F/S ON 2:45 HOLD 2:35
DRILL:	100 BK OR IM
SWIM:	4 X 300 IM (75 EACH STROKE) ON 5:00 HOLD 4:45
SPRINT:	4 X 50 F/S
HOLD:	38 SWIM:DOWN EZ 200 STROKE

73. Mastering

SWIM:	500 YDS EZ ALL 4 STROKES
SWIM:	12 X 25 ON :30 IM ORDER
SWIM:	8 X 25 F/S ON :25
KICK:	8 X 75 ALTERNATE F/S AND STROKE ON 1:30
DRILL:	200 BR (2 KICKS TO 1 PULL)
SWIM:	200 F/S BUILD FROM :45/:50 TO :40/:50 *REST 30 SEC*
SWIM:	4 X 200 F/S ON 2:45 HOLD 2:35
DRILL:	100 BK OR IM
SWIM:	4 X 300 IM (75 EACH STROKE) ON 5:00 HOLD 4:45
SPRINT:	4 X 50 F/S
HOLD:	38 SWIM:DOWN EZ 200 STROKE

The world makes way for a determined person.

158. Mastering

SWIM:	500 YDS EZ WARM UP
SWIM:	10 X 50 BEST STROKE ON 1:15
KICK:	8 X 100
	ALTERNATE F/S AND CHOICE ON 2:00
DRILL:	4 X 25 IM ORDER WITH 5 SEC REST
PULL:	4 X (100 IM + 100 STROKE) ON 3:45
	USE IM ORDER FOR STROKES
SWIM:	500 F/S ON 7:00
	CHECK 400 TIME *REST 30 SEC*
SWIM:	400 F/S BETTER THAN PREVIOUS TIME
	CHECK 300 TIME *REST 30 SEC*
SWIM:	300 F/S BETTER THAN PREVIOUS TIME
	CHECK 200 TIME *REST 30 SEC*
SWIM:	200 F/S BETTER THAN PREVIOUS TIME
	CHECK 100 TIME *REST 30 SEC*
SWIM:	100 F/S BETTER THAN PREVIOUS TIME
	CHECK 50 TIME *REST 30 SEC*
SWIM:	50 F/S FAST !
SWIM:	DOWN EZ 200 CHOICE

74. Mastering

SWIM:	500 YDS F/S AND 1 STROKE EZ
KICK:	6 X 100 ALTERNATE STROKE AND F/S ON 2:00
SWIM:	12 X 25 FLY ON :30 *BREATHE EVERY 3*
PULL:	(200 BR + 200 F/S) ON 7:00
SWIM:	12 X 75 BK ON 1:30 HOLD 1:13
SWIM:	400 F/S *GOOD TECHNIQUE* ON 5:45
DRILL:	8 X (50 FLY ON 1:10, SWIM 25 FLY FAST ON :35)
SPRINT:	4 X 25 F/S ON :45 *NO BREATHE FOR LAST 10 YDS*
SWIM:	DOWN EZ 200 STROKE

74. Mastering

SWIM:	500 YDS F/S AND 1 STROKE EZ
KICK:	6 X 100 ALTERNATE STROKE AND F/S ON 2:00
SWIM:	12 X 25 FLY ON :30 *BREATHE EVERY 3*
PULL:	(200 BR + 200 F/S) ON 7:00
SWIM:	12 X 75 BK ON 1:30 HOLD 1:13
SWIM:	400 F/S *GOOD TECHNIQUE* ON 5:45
DRILL:	8 X (50 FLY ON 1:10, SWIM 25 FLY FAST ON :35)
SPRINT:	4 X 25 F/S ON :45 *NO BREATHE FOR LAST 10 YDS*
SWIM:	DOWN EZ 200 STROKE

Try? Try not! Do or do not.
Yoda

159. Mastering

SWIM:	500 YDS EZ CHOICE
KICK:	400 IM ON 8:00
	16 X 25 ON :30
	ALTERNATE F/S AND BR
PULL:	3 X 200 F/S ON 3:00
	BREATHE 3,5 PER 100
SWIM:	4 X 50 FLY ON 1:00 FAST
	200 F/S *FOR TECHNIQUE*
	6 X 50 BK ON 1:15 FAST
	200 BR *FOR TECHNIQUE*
	8 X 50 BR ON 1:30 FAST
	200 BK *FOR TECHNIQUE*
	10 X 50 F/S ON 1:00 HOLD :35
SWIM:	DOWN EZ 200 F/S

75. Mastering

SWIM: 500 YDS EZ F/S WARM UP
KICK: 6 X 100 CHOICE ON 2:05
PULL: 200 BK + 100 BR + 200 F/S
SWIM: 4 X 25 FLY WITH *5 SEC REST*
+ 100 FLY + *10 SEC REST*
4 X 25 BK WITH *5 SEC REST*
+ 100 BK + *10 SEC REST*
4 X 25 BR WITH 5 SEC REST
+ 100 BR + *10 SEC REST*
4 X 25 F/S WITH 5 SEC REST + 100 F/S
SWIM: 12 X 50 F/S ON :45 SWIM AT 500 PACE
SWIM: 3 X 200 BK ON 3:30
SWIM: 4 X 100 BR ON 2:00
SWIM: 4 X 25 FLY ON :30 *BREATHE 3*
SWIM: DOWN EZ 200 F/S

75. Mastering

SWIM: 500 YDS EZ F/S WARM UP
KICK: 6 X 100 CHOICE ON 2:05
PULL: 200 BK + 100 BR + 200 F/S
SWIM: 4 X 25 FLY WITH *5 SEC REST*
+ 100 FLY + *10 SEC REST*
4 X 25 BK WITH *5 SEC REST*
+ 100 BK + *10 SEC REST*
4 X 25 BR WITH 5 SEC REST
+ 100 BR + *10 SEC REST*
4 X 25 F/S WITH 5 SEC REST + 100 F/S
SWIM: 12 X 50 F/S ON :45 SWIM AT 500 PACE
SWIM: 3 X 200 BK ON 3:30
SWIM: 4 X 100 BR ON 2:00
SWIM: 4 X 25 FLY ON :30 *BREATHE 3*
SWIM: DOWN EZ 200 F/S

If I cannot do great things, I 'll do small things in a great way.

160. Mastering

SWIM:	500 YDS EZ F/S
SWIM:	10 X 50 F/S ON :50 HOLD:37
KICK:	6 X 100 REVERSE IM ON 2:00
DRILL:	100 BK DOUBLE ARM
PULL:	6 X (75 F/S + 25 STROKE) ON 1:45
SWIM:	8 X (50 F/S + 50 STROKE + 50 F/S) ON 2 :15 IM ORDER OR CHOICE OF STROKE
SWIM:	4 X 100 WORST STROKE ON 2 :15 *IMPROVING TECHNIQUE*
SWIM:	DOWN EZ 200 STROKE

76. Mastering

SWIM:	500 YDS EZ, 2 STROKES, CHOICE
DRILL:	100 IM
PULL:	16 X 75 ON 1:15 ALTERNATE BK AND F/S
SWIM:	3 X 200 F/S ON 2:45 + 200 IM ON 3:45 2 X 200 F/S ON 2:50 + 2 X 100 IM ON 1:45 1 X 200 F/S ON 2:55 HOLD 2:40 FOR ALL 200 F/S
KICK:	200 FLY + 100 BK + 100 BR + 200 F/S
SPRINT:	4 X 25 FLY OR BR ON :45
SWIM:	DOWN EZ 200 STROKE

76. Mastering

SWIM:	500 YDS EZ, 2 STROKES, CHOICE
DRILL:	100 IM
PULL:	16 X 75 ON 1:15 ALTERNATE BK AND F/S
SWIM:	3 X 200 F/S ON 2:45 + 200 IM ON 3:45 2 X 200 F/S ON 2:50 + 2 X 100 IM ON 1:45 1 X 200 F/S ON 2:55 HOLD 2:40 FOR ALL 200 F/S
KICK:	200 FLY + 100 BK + 100 BR + 200 F/S
SPRINT:	4 X 25 FLY OR BR ON :45
SWIM:	DOWN EZ 200 STROKE

Old swimmers never die; they just go off their blocks.

161. Mastering

SWIM:	500 YDS CHOICE WARM UP
SWIM:	4 X (75 F/S ON 1:05 + 50 F/S ON :40 + 25 F/S ON:30)
PULL:	100 + 200 + 300 F/S *WITH 10 SEC REST BETWEEN* *BREATHE 5*
KICK:	5 X 100 CHOICE ON 2:00
DRILL:	4 X 25 IM ORDER ON :30
SWIM:	16 X 25 FLY ON :40
	16 X 25 BK ON :30
	16 X 25 BR ON :40
	16 X 25 F/S ON :25
SWIM:	400 IM MODERATE FOR TECHNIQUE
SWIM:	DOWN EZ 200 F/S

77. Mastering

SWIM:	500 YDS EZ F/S WARM UP
KICK:	10 X (50 F/S + 25 CHOICE) ON 1:30
DRILL:	6 X 25 BK ON :30 DOUBLE ARM
SWIM:	2 X 200 BK ON 3:30
SWIM:	4 X (3 X 25 F/S ON :25) + (1 X 25 BEST STROKE ON :30)
PULL:	3 X (250 F/S + 50 BR) ON 5:00
SWIM:	2 X 200 BR ON 3:30
SWIM:	8 X 75 F/S ON 1:15 HOLD :57
SWIM:	DOWN EZ 200 CHOICE

77. Mastering

SWIM:	500 YDS EZ F/S WARM UP
KICK:	10 X (50 F/S + 25 CHOICE) ON 1:30
DRILL:	6 X 25 BK ON :30 DOUBLE ARM
SWIM:	2 X 200 BK ON 3:30
SWIM:	4 X (3 X 25 F/S ON :25) + (1 X 25 BEST STROKE ON :30)
PULL:	3 X (250 F/S + 50 BR) ON 5:00
SWIM:	2 X 200 BR ON 3:30
SWIM:	8 X 75 F/S ON 1:15 HOLD :57
SWIM:	DOWN EZ 200 CHOICE

To excuse yourself is to accuse yourself.

162. Mastering

SWIM:	500 YDS F/S EZ WARM UP WITH DRILLS
SWIM:	12 X 50 ON 1:00, AS 3 OF EACH STROKE
KICK:	8 X 75 IM ON 1:30
	OMIT A STROKE EACH TIME
PULL:	4 X 150 F/S ON 2:15 FAST
SWIM:	2 X (50 FLY + 50 F/S) ON 2:10 *QUALITY*
	2 X (50 FLY + 50 BK) ON 2:10 *QUALITY*
	2 X (50 BK + 50 BR) ON 2:10 *QUALITY*
	2 X (50 BR + 50 F/S) ON 2:10 *QUALITY*
SWIM:	75 F/S ON 1:05 +
	125 F/S ON 1:50 +
	175 F/S ON 2:25 +
	225 F/S ON 3:15
SPRINT:	4 X 75 STROKE ON 1:15
	4 X 25 STROKE ON :40 FAST !
SWIM:	DOWN EZ 200 CHOICE

78. Mastering

SWIM: 10 X 50 F/S WITH *10 SEC REST* WARM UP
PULL: 8 X (100 F/S + 25 BR) ON 1:55
KICK: 500 EZ 25/HARD 25 - CHOICE
SWIM: 6 X (50 FLY +
50 BK KICK +
50 BR +
50 F/S KICK) ON 3:45
SWIM: 3 X 300 BK OR BR ON 5:15
SWIM: 24 X 25 F/S
ON :20, :25 ,:30 REPEATING
SWIM: DOWN EZ 200 F/S

78. Mastering

SWIM: 10 X 50 F/S WITH *10 SEC REST* WARM UP
PULL: 8 X (100 F/S + 25 BR) ON 1:55
KICK: 500 EZ 25/HARD 25 - CHOICE
SWIM: 6 X (50 FLY +
50 BK KICK +
50 BR +
50 F/S KICK) ON 3:45
SWIM: 3 X 300 BK OR BR ON 5:15
SWIM: 24 X 25 F/S
ON :20, :25 ,:30 REPEATING
SWIM: DOWN EZ 200 F/S

Unless my lungs burn and I can hardly drag myself from the pool, I know I haven't had a workout.
Murray Rose

163. Mastering

SWIM:	500 YDS EZ USING ALL STROKES
SWIM:	18 X 25 F/S ALTERNATE
	ON :20, :25, :30
KICK:	5 X 100 CHOICE
	ON 2:05 NEGATIVE SPLIT
PULL:	2 X (100 BK + 200 F/S + 50 BR)
	ON 6:00
SWIM:	500 F/S ON 7:00
	2 X 200 F/S ON 3:00
	10 X 50 F/S ON :45
	20 X 25 F/S ON :30
SWIM:	DOWN EZ 200 F/S

79. Mastering

SWIM:	500 YDS F/S EZ WARM UP
SWIM:	4 X (25 ON :20, 50 ON :40, 75 ON 1:10 F/S)
KICK:	8 X 75 CHOICE ON 1:30
DRILL:	200 IM
PULL:	500 USE ALL 4 STROKES
SWIM:	10 X 100 IM ON 1:45
SPRINT:	3 X 50 F/S ON :40
	4 X 50 F/S ON :45
	5 X 50 F/S ON :50
	INCREASE SPEED WITH REST
SWIM:	DOWN EZ 200 STROKE AND F/S

79. Mastering

SWIM:	500 YDS F/S EZ WARM UP
SWIM:	4 X (25 ON :20, 50 ON :40, 75 ON 1:10 F/S)
KICK:	8 X 75 CHOICE ON 1:30
DRILL:	200 IM
PULL:	500 USE ALL 4 STROKES
SWIM:	10 X 100 IM ON 1:45
SPRINT:	3 X 50 F/S ON :40
	4 X 50 F/S ON :45
	5 X 50 F/S ON :50
	INCREASE SPEED WITH REST
SWIM:	DOWN EZ 200 STROKE AND F/S

How did a fool and his money get together in the first place?

164. Mastering

SWIM:	500 YDS F/S LONG ~ EZ WARM UP
SWIM:	5 X 50 F/S ON :50
	5 X 50 F/S ON :45
KICK:	600 IM AS 4 X 150
PULL:	4 X 200 F/S
	WITH LAST 50 STROKE OF IM
	ON 3:30
SWIM:	8 X (50 FLY + 50 F/S) ON 2:15
SWIM:	4 X 200 ON 4:00 ALTERNATE BK ~ BR
	OR
	4 X 300 F/S ON 4:10
SPRINT:	4 X 25 IM ORDER ON 2:00
	WITH EZ 25 F/S AFTER EACH
SWIM:	DOWN EZ 200 STROKE

80. Mastering

SWIM:	500 YDS USING ALL 4 STROKES
SWIM:	8 X 50 F/S ON :40
KICK:	4 X 150 CHOICE USING 2 STROKES ON 3:30
PULL:	4 X (100 BR + 100 F/S) ON 4 :15
SWIM:	4 X (50 FLY + 100 BK) ON 2:45
	4 X (50 BK + 200 F/S) ON 4 :15
DRILL:	(DRILL 25, SWIM 50) X 4 IM ORDER ON 1:30
SWIM:	DOWN EZ 200 F/S

80. Mastering

SWIM:	500 YDS USING ALL 4 STROKES
SWIM:	8 X 50 F/S ON :40
KICK:	4 X 150 CHOICE USING 2 STROKES ON 3:30
PULL:	4 X (100 BR + 100 F/S) ON 4 :15
SWIM:	4 X (50 FLY + 100 BK) ON 2:45
	4 X (50 BK + 200 F/S) ON 4 :15
DRILL:	(DRILL 25, SWIM 50) X 4 IM ORDER ON 1:30
SWIM:	DOWN EZ 200 F/S

There is a big difference between wanting to and willing to.

165. Mastering

SWIM:	500 YDS F/S AND STROKE EZ WARM UP
DRILL:	SWIM 400 IM
SWIM:	6 X 75 F/S ON 1:05
PULL:	5 X 100 IM ON 2:00
KICK:	200 BK + 200 BR + 200 F/S
DRILL:	100 CHOICE
SWIM:	4 X 175 F/S ON 2:40
SWIM:	200 BK FOR TIME
SWIM:	200 BR EZ ON 4 :15 200 BR HARD FOR TIME
SWIM:	10 X 25 F/S ON :30 *NO BREATHE LAST 10 YDS*
SWIM:	DOWN EZ 200 F/S

81. Mastering

SWIM: 500 YDS F/S EZ
KICK: 8 X 75 F/S ON 1:20
DRILL: 4 X 25 IM ORDER ON :30
SWIM: 16 X 25 F/S ON :25
PULL: 10 X 100
ALTERNATE F/S AND STROKE
ON 1:45
SWIM: 3 X (100 F/S EZ ON 2:00 +
200 STROKE ON 3:30)
USE FLY, BK, BR FOR STROKE IN
THAT ORDER
SWIM: 5 X 50 STROKE ON :55
5 X 50 F/S ON :45 HOLD :35
SWIM: DOWN EZ 200 STROKE

81. Mastering

SWIM: 500 YDS F/S EZ
KICK: 8 X 75 F/S ON 1:20
DRILL: 4 X 25 IM ORDER ON :30
SWIM: 16 X 25 F/S ON :25
PULL: 10 X 100
ALTERNATE F/S AND STROKE
ON 1:45
SWIM: 3 X (100 F/S EZ ON 2:00 +
200 STROKE ON 3:30)
USE FLY, BK, BR FOR STROKE IN
THAT ORDER
SWIM: 5 X 50 STROKE ON :55
5 X 50 F/S ON :45 HOLD :35
SWIM: DOWN EZ 200 STROKE

Success is never final, and failure is never fatal; it's determination which counts.

166. Mastering

SWIM:	500 YDS EZ STROKES WARM UP
KICK:	4 X (50 EZ + 50 FAST) IM ORDER ON 2 :10
KICK:	2 X (50 EZ + 50 FAST) FLY-ON-BACK & F/S ON 2 :15
PULL:	6 X 100 F/S ON 1:45 + 200 BR
SWIM:	6 X (50 FLY + 50 BK) ON 1:50
SWIM:	6 X (25 FLY + 25 BK + 50 BR) ON 1:50
SWIM:	6 X 100 IM ON 1:50
SPRINT:	8 X 30 YDS (INCLUDES FAST TURN) ON 1:00
SWIM:	DOWN EZ 200 F/S

82. Mastering

SWIM:	500 YDS EZ WARM UP
	USE 3 STROKES
SWIM:	8 X 50 F/S ON :45
KICK:	10 X 50 CHOICE ON :55
PULL:	4 X (100 STROKE + 100 F/S) ON 3:30
SWIM:	8 X 100 IM ON 1:45
SWIM:	8 X 50 FLY ON 1:00
	8 X 75 BK ON 1:15
	8 X 25 BR ON :30
	8 X 50 F/S ON 1:00
	BREATHE 5
SWIM:	DOWN EZ 200 STROKE

82. Mastering

SWIM:	500 YDS EZ WARM UP
	USE 3 STROKES
SWIM:	8 X 50 F/S ON :45
KICK:	10 X 50 CHOICE ON :55
PULL:	4 X (100 STROKE + 100 F/S) ON 3:30
SWIM:	8 X 100 IM ON 1:45
SWIM:	8 X 50 FLY ON 1:00
	8 X 75 BK ON 1:15
	8 X 25 BR ON :30
	8 X 50 F/S ON 1:00
	BREATHE 5
SWIM:	DOWN EZ 200 STROKE

The worst bankruptcy is the person who has lost enthusiasm.

167. Mastering

SWIM:	500 YDS F/S EZ
SWIM:	6 X 100 IM ON 1:45
KICK:	3 X 200 CHOICE, IM, CHOICE ON 4:25
PULL:	500 F/S *BREATHE 3, 5, 3, 5, 3 PER 100*
SWIM:	10 X 50 FLY OR BK ON 1:00 10 X 50 BR OR F/S ON 1:00 10 X 50 F/S ON :50 8 X 50 IM ORDER ON 1:00
SWIM:	DOWN EZ 200 STROKE

83 .Mastering

SWIM:	4 X 125 CHOICE ON 2:00
KICK:	3 X 200 IM ON 4:00
DRILL:	4 X 25 IM ORDER ON :30
SWIM:	10 X (50 F/S ON :45, 25 F/S ON :25)
PULL:	5 X (150 F/S + 50 BR) ON 3:30
SWIM:	5 X (25 FLY + 175 BK) ON 3:30
SWIM:	4 X (75 BR + 100 F/S) ON 2:45
SWIM:	DOWN EZ 200 CHOICE

83 .Mastering

SWIM:	4 X 125 CHOICE ON 2:00
KICK:	3 X 200 IM ON 4:00
DRILL:	4 X 25 IM ORDER ON :30
SWIM:	10 X (50 F/S ON :45, 25 F/S ON :25)
PULL:	5 X (150 F/S + 50 BR) ON 3:30
SWIM:	5 X (25 FLY + 175 BK) ON 3:30
SWIM:	4 X (75 BR + 100 F/S) ON 2:45
SWIM:	DOWN EZ 200 CHOICE

Sleep and rest is the heart of good training.

168. Mastering

SWIM:	500 YDS
	USE F/S AND 2 STROKES
	EZ WARM UP
SWIM:	8 X 75 F/S ALTERNATE ON 1:00, 1:10
	HARD AND THEN EZ
KICK:	20 X 25 ON :30 CHOICE - BUILD
PULL:	8 X (25 BR + 50 F/S) ON 1:15
SWIM:	6 X (50 FLY + 100 BK + 50 F/S)
	ON 3:30
DRILL:	200 IM
SPRINT:	8 X 50 F/S ON 1:15 HOLD:34
SWIM:	DOWN EZ 200 F/S

84. Mastering

SWIM:	500 YDS F/S EZ WARM UP
SWIM:	16 X 25 F/S ALTERNATE ON :20 AND :25
KICK:	12 X 50 CHOICE ON :55
PULL:	5 X (25 STROKE + 50 BR + 125 F/S) ON 3:30
SWIM:	(100 FLY + 5 SEC + 50 FLY + 5 SEC + 200 BACK + 200 BR + 200 F/S) X 2 ON 14:00
SWIM:	4 X 25 F/S ON :40 NO BREATH
SWIM:	DOWN EZ 200 F/S

84. Mastering

SWIM:	500 YDS F/S EZ WARM UP
SWIM:	16 X 25 F/S ALTERNATE ON :20 AND :25
KICK:	12 X 50 CHOICE ON :55
PULL:	5 X (25 STROKE + 50 BR + 125 F/S) ON 3:30
SWIM:	(100 FLY + 5 SEC + 50 FLY + 5 SEC + 200 BACK + 200 BR + 200 F/S) X 2 ON 14:00
SWIM:	4 X 25 F/S ON :40 NO BREATH
SWIM:	DOWN EZ 200 F/S

The key to being an expert is to complicate the simple.

169. Mastering

SWIM:	500 YDS EZ F/S AND DRILLS
SWIM:	200 STROKE ON 3:45
KICK:	100 BK ON 2:00
PULL:	400 F/S ON 6:00
SWIM:	200 IM ON 3:30
	REPEAT ABOVE SET AS SWIM/KICK/PULL/SWIM 4 TIMES
KICK:	400 REVERSE IM ON 8:15
DRILL:	200 F/S
SWIM:	8 X 150 F/S ON 2:15
	DESCEND 1-4, AND 5-8
SWIM:	DOWN EZ 200 CHOICE

85. Mastering

SWIM: 500 YDS EZ USE BK AND F/S
SWIM: 11 X 400 YDS F/S ON 5:45
TRY TO HOLD 5:30
SWIM: DOWN EZ 200 STROKE

85. Mastering

SWIM: 500 YDS EZ USE BK AND F/S
SWIM: 11 X 400 YDS F/S ON 5:45
TRY TO HOLD 5:30
SWIM: DOWN EZ 200 STROKE

Age, cunning, deceit, and treachery can defeat youth and skill.

A Master Swimmer's T-shirt

170. Mastering

SWIM:	500 YDS CHOICE WARM UP
SWIM:	4 X (50 BK + 100 BR + 50 F/S) ON 3:45
KICK:	200 BK ON 4:10
	8 X 50 CHOICE ON 1:00
PULL:	4 X (125 F/S + 50 BR) ON 3:00 *BREATHE EVERY 3 ON F/S AND EVERY 2 ON BR*
SWIM:	8 X 50 F/S FAST ON 1:15
SWIM:	8 X 75 STROKE ON 1:30
SPRINT:	4 X (25 F/S + TURN) ON :44 *NO BREATHERS*
SWIM:	DOWN EZ 200 F/S